THE 'LITTLE' NOR
WESTERN RAILW

Skipton – Lancaster – Morecambe – Heysham
Clapham – Ingleton – Low Gill

Martin Bairstow

Compound 4-4-0 No 41004 approaching Hellifield with a Morecambe to Leeds express about 1949.
(J.W. Hague, courtesy of David Beeken)

Published by Martin Bairstow, 53 Kirklees Drive, Farsley, Leeds
Printed by Amadeus Press, Cleckheaton, West Yorkshire

Introduction

The North Western Railway was incorporated in 1846 to connect Skipton, on the soon to be opened Leeds & Bradford Extension Railway, with Lancaster and Low Gill on the Lancaster & Carlisle Railway which was also then under construction. The unofficial prefix 'Little' was a term of endearment (or possibly abuse) to distinguish this enterprise from the somewhat larger London & North Western Railway which had been incorporated about the same time.

Despite financial difficulties, the Company was able to complete the Skipton to Lancaster route fairly quickly. In contrast, the Low Gill line proved more of a problem. The 'Little' North Western failed in the task which had to be completed by the London & North Western Railway – part of a series of events which provoked the Midland Railway into promoting, and then actually building, the Settle & Carlisle Line.

Also incorporated in 1846 was the Morecambe Railway & Harbour Company. This was taken over by the 'Little' North Western before work had even begun. The 'Little' North Western thus became involved in steamer traffic out of Morecambe. Half a century later, its successor the Midland Railway went on to build the harbour complex at Heysham.

Today the railway still functions between Skipton, Lancaster and Morecambe but is something of a backwater with no freight traffic and just a modest passenger service. It suffers badly from a detour imposed during the Beeching Period.

In 1975 Heysham lost its remaining passenger service, both rail and ship, but since then it has experienced something of a revival. It is now the main port for the Isle of Man. In March 1999 it regained a service to Belfast courtesy of a new generation of fast ferry.

This book traces the story of the 'Little' North Western Railway and its associated shipping interests from the beginnings up to the present day.

I am grateful to everybody who has helped with the book. The photographs are credited individually. The text was typed by Glynis, Jayne and Jean at Sutcliffe & Riley, Chartered Accountants. The excursion leaflets came from David Beeken. The tickets were from the collection of our late friend, Geoffrey Lewthwaite, kindly loaned by Jeanne before they were sold. Alan Young lettered the maps. Richard Pulleyn drew the signal diagrams. John Holroyd removed blemishes from some of the photographs. I must acknowledge delving into *North of Leeds* by Peter E. Baughan for some of the historical background.

Farsley, Leeds — Martin Bairstow
August 2000

'Black Five' 4-6-0 No 44904 leaving Skipton for the 'Little' North Western line on 22 June 1964. *(Peter E. Baughan)*

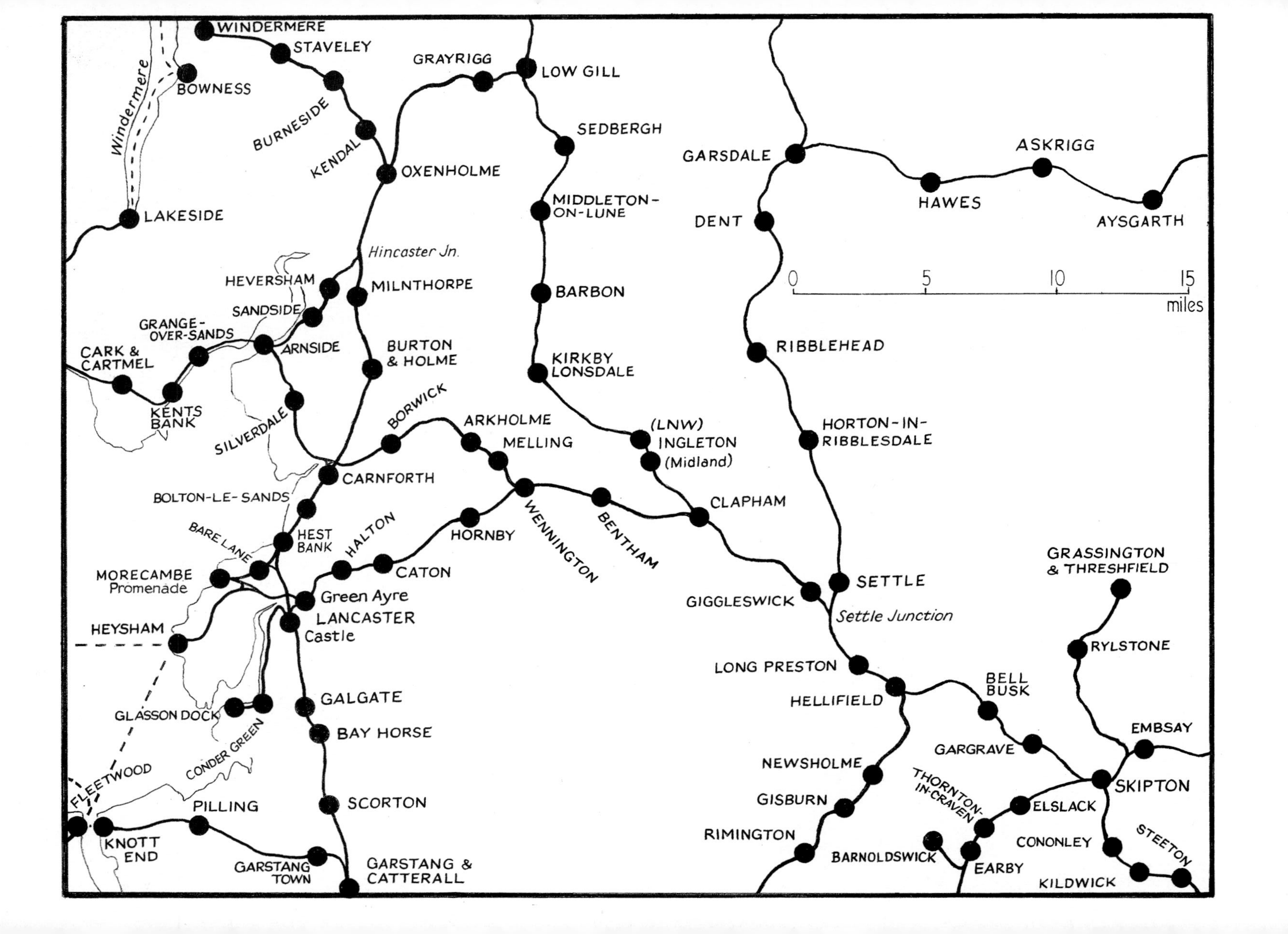

WINDERMERE
STAVELEY
BOWNESS
Windermere
BURNESIDE
KENDAL
GRAYRIGG
LOW GILL
OXENHOLME
SEDBERGH
LAKESIDE
MIDDLETON-ON-LUNE
GARSDALE
DENT
ASKRIGG
HAWES
AYSGARTH
0
5
10
15
miles
Hincaster Jn.
HEVERSHAM
MILNTHORPE
BARBON
SANDSIDE
GRANGE-OVER-SANDS
CARK & CARTMEL
ARNSIDE
BURTON & HOLME
KIRKBY LONSDALE
RIBBLEHEAD
KENTS BANK
SILVERDALE
BORWICK
ARKHOLME
MELLING
(LNW)
INGLETON
(Midland)
HORTON-IN-RIBBLESDALE
CARNFORTH
BOLTON-LE-SANDS
WENNINGTON
BENTHAM
CLAPHAM
BARE LANE
HEST BANK
HALTON
HORNBY
CATON
MORECAMBE
Promenade
Green Ayre
LANCASTER
Castle
HEYSHAM
GIGGLESWICK
SETTLE
Settle Junction
GRASSINGTON & THRESHFIELD
RYLSTONE
LONG PRESTON
HELLIFIELD
BELL BUSK
GALGATE
GLASSON DOCK
BAY HORSE
CONDER GREEN
FLEETWOOD
PILLING
SCORTON
KNOTT END
GARSTANG TOWN
GARSTANG & CATTERALL
NEWSHOLME
GISBURN
RIMINGTON
GARGRAVE
EMBSAY
SKIPTON
THORNTON-IN-CRAVEN
ELSLACK
BARNOLDSWICK
EARBY
CONONLEY
STEETON
KILDWICK

A trip to the Seaside

142083 pauses at Skipton whilst I get Philippa a coffee, 16 January 1999.
(Martin Bairstow)

Saturday 16 January 1999, 10.49am. 142095 working the 10.17 Leeds–Morecambe pulls into platform 3 at Skipton. The conductor announces that there will be a short break before it leaves again at 10.55. We've been on since Shipley.

Philippa is desperate for a coffee and persuades me to sprint under the subway to the newly refurbished main building where I can procure her one either from a machine or from the buffet. I accomplish the mission with sufficient margin to take the accompanying photograph.

Skipton Station opened on its present site on 1 May 1876, the day that passenger services began over the Settle & Carlisle Line. It comprises three long through platforms plus a bay at the Bradford end. Platforms 5 and 6 were added when the Ilkley line opened in 1888. They have been disused and subway access bricked off since the Ilkley line closed in 1965. Quarry trains still use the first two miles of the Ilkley line on their way to Rylstone on the truncated Grassington branch.

Skipton declined further with withdrawal of the Bradford trains in 1965 and closure of the Colne line in 1970. Track was removed from the bay platform 1 whilst platform 4 was reduced to a carriage siding.

When the track layout was remodelled and resignalled in 1994, in anticipation of electrification, all four platforms were brought back into use. In 1998 passenger facilities were improved with the opening of a new travel centre in the main building adjoining platform 2. At the same time, the entire station was repainted including the remaining ironwork.

Punctually at 10.55, we pull away from Skipton. To our left the remains of the engine shed, closed in April 1967. To our right the sidings where today's electric and diesel multiple units are stabled.

Just before the bypass bridge, we take a curve to the right. This was Skipton North Junction where our route used to diverge from the Colne line which continued straight on, its path now blocked by the bypass. Beyond, we can see the Colne line continuing on an embankment which is broken where the bridge has been removed over the River Aire. For many years there was a speed restriction on our own bridge over the River Aire but this has been replaced by a new span so now we can progress at normal speed.

The first stop is Gargrave which has benefited from Railtrack's station refurbishment programme. No longer are steps required to board the train. 'Little' North Western stone shelters survive on each platform. So does the main wooden building but that is now in private use.

A similar building survives as a restaurant at Bell Busk which closed in 1959. It used to be advertised as the station for Malham, four miles away. Malham is the source of the River Aire which flows towards the North Sea. In the next three miles we pass through the Aire Gap, a break in the Pennines. At Hellifield we are in the valley of the Ribble which flows towards the Irish Sea.

Opened on the present site in 1880, Hellifield Station is on a scale out of all proportion to the modest traffic of a relatively small village. Hellifield was the junction with the Lancashire & Yorkshire Railway whose traffic from Manchester and Liverpool joined the Settle & Carlisle line here. At present there are just two passenger trains per week, summer only, coming off the L&Y route, both of them on Sundays. It is a measure of how the tide has turned on railway closures that, in 1962, the Blackburn to Hellifield service was withdrawn with no apparent concern for hardship to users. Yet in

Skipton Station North Junction, 13 August 1992. The box closed on Saturday 22 October 1994. *(F.W. Smith)*

The lever frame at Skipton Station North Junction. *(F.W. Smith)*

'Black Five' No. 44906 doing a spot of bridge inspection at Broughton in Craven, between Skipton and Gargrave on 25 April 1965. *(Martin Bairstow Collection)*

1989, the Secretary of State for Transport refused closure of the same route, then used only by a handful of excursion trains per annum. It is as well that he did. The line is now earmarked by Railtrack as part of an Anglo-Scottish freight route.

Today's stopping trains use only the Leeds end of the large island platform at Hellifield. The rest of the station, including the buildings, has been restored and tenanted. On the left hand side of the line is a part completed shed upon which work appears to have come to a standstill. This was intended as a visitor centre. Access to it is afforded by a new road from a junction with the A65 about ½ mile towards Settle. This road is built to a high standard, as far as it goes but, as with the shed, work seems to have been suspended. *(This was still the case over a year later).*

The West Coast Railway Company, operator of the summer steam train between Fort William and Mallaig, has ambitions for a regular steam service between Hellifield and Carlisle. A steam running shed would be built on the site of the old shed which stood to the right hand side of the station as we look towards Settle Junction.

Critics of the privatised railway sometimes say that Railtrack doesn't invest in the network, it merely spends (or just wastes) money to impress the Regulator. Long Preston Station is the proof of this theory. In 1997 they resurfaced the platforms at the old inadequate height. Apparently they intend to raise the height (and thus obliterate the new surface) in the near future.

At Settle Junction we must slow down to negotiate the 15mph single lead junction. This was installed following damage to the previous double track junction in an accident on 3 May 1979.

For 12 months after the opening of the Carlisle line, there was a station at Settle Junction. This was in addition to Settle (on the Carlisle line) and Settle Old on the 'Little' North Western. It was probably intended to close Settle Old but, instead, the Midland Railway decided to retain this station under the name Giggleswick and dispense with the Junction Station. Though closed in 1877, the main building, in standard Settle & Carlisle style, remained in situ until the 1960s.

We have now left the Leeds–Settle–Carlisle route to traverse a line which has become something of a backwater. Once clear of Settle Junction, we are again on double track but, such is the density of traffic, that there is just one block section all the way to Carnforth Station Junction a distance of 24½ miles. The track is in poor condition and there are a number of speed restrictions below the general line limit of 60mph.

We are bouncing along on No.142095, a two-car 'pacer' unit built in the mid 1980s. At that time, the politics of new rolling stock was that it had to be cheap – or at least appear cheap – even if it was expensive to build.

The class 142 was a development – and quite an advance – from the 140 and 141 which were put

The 14.35 Leeds–Morecambe, 53621 leading, has been running hot and is taking water under the Midland canopy at Hellifield on 21 September 1983. *(Tom Heavyside)*

Inside our refurbished class 142. *(Martin Bairstow)*

New platform surface at Long Preston – a lesson in how to waste money? – or just stupidity? *(Martin Bairstow)*

The remains of Settle Junction Station, closed since 1877, seen from a northbound passing train on 3 September 1964. *(Peter E. Baughan)*

156490 negotiates the single lead junction at Settle Junction on a Morecambe to Leeds journey in August 1997. *(David Beeken)*

Traditional block instruments still in use at Settle Junction in August 1997. *(David Beeken)*

Settle Junction 11 March 1989. 20120 and 20090 head a train of steel coil from Ravenscraig to Dee Marsh, diverted via Hellifield because of engineering work on the main line south of Lancaster. *(Tom Heavyside)*

Wennington Junction for Carnforth and Furness Stations, 11 October 1958. *(J.C.W. Halliday)*

together from standard bus parts. Our two carriages are each carried on only four wheels, despite the widespread introduction of bogie (8 wheel stock) more than a hundred years ago. This particular set has recently been refurbished with superior seating to the previous bus seats. It has not yet been repainted externally in the new Northern Spirit livery.

Giggleswick Station is a rather spartan affair with low platforms and no footbridge. All the buildings have gone. Pedestrian access involves risking one's life crossing the Settle bypass. The pub on the other side of this highway is still called 'The Old Station'.

By early 2000, the station regeneration programme was in full swing at Giggleswick, Clapham and Wennington.

Clapham retains a 'Little' North Western stone shelter. The main wooden building stands alongside the Leeds bound platform but is now in private ownership. Just beyond the station, the line curves to the left at what used to be Clapham Junction. Straight ahead you can see the abandoned formation heading towards Ingleton. It is clear which was laid out as the main line and which the branch. We follow the branch.

The main building at Bentham, on the Skipton bound platform, has a 1950s air. It is out of railway use but murals have been painted in the windows to brighten the place up. The village here is High Bentham. When the line opened there was a station also at Low Bentham. This closed to passengers in 1853 but there remained a goods yard, the site of which we can just make out on the right.

Pulling away from Wennington Station, we pass a signal box still proclaiming the name Wennington Junction. Inside, most of the levers are white, that is out of use. In fact the box has been permanently switched out for many years but could be opened to split the Settle Junction to Carnforth block in the event of an emergency or sudden upsurge in traffic.

We are only $10\frac{3}{4}$ miles from Lancaster and $14\frac{3}{4}$ from Morecambe – at least this would be the case had Dr Beeching not sent us on a rather fruitless diversion. Curving to the right, away from the former junction, we can see the embankment of the original 'Little' North Western heading direct towards Lancaster. We enter Melling Tunnel, 1,230 yards in length, then pass through Melling the first of three closed stations on this, the Furness & Midland Joint Line. We are travelling north west, at right angles to where we ought to be going. Two miles beyond Arkholme, we make a sharp turn to the left as we enter the valley of the River Keer. We suffer two speed restrictions on bridges, one over the Keer, the other over the Lancaster Canal. We go under the M6, one of the earliest stretches of motorway to be built. Then we pass over the electrified West Coast Main Line before coming to the recently closed Carnforth East Junction signal box *(since demolished)*. The tracks continuing straight on towards Barrow have been severed. Our two 4 wheel coaches screech badly as we take the

10mph sharp left hand curve into Carnforth. To our right is the motive power depot, still with coaling tower. Since the demise of BR steam in 1968, Carnforth has been a base for preserved locomotives and rolling stock.

Carnforth Station is the biggest disappointment of the whole journey. When the Leeds–Morecambe trains were re-routed this way in 1966, we were promised that Carnforth would be the place to make connections with the West Coast Main Line. Yet in 1970, the main line platforms were closed and later demolished. Since 1990, the station has been unstaffed. Passengers enter through the old boarded up booking hall and must walk along the fenced off up main line platform to reach the subway which leads to the former Furness platforms where every doorway and window is also boarded up. The only relief from the dereliction is a small plaque on the wall recording that the film 'Brief Encounter' was filmed in a refreshment room here in 1945. It is possible that this link with the silver screen may assist in raising a funding package to restore the surviving half of the station.

It is hard to credit that, as rebuilt in 1880, Carnforth Station had an overall roof. This was removed in the late 1930s prior to construction of the present platform 2 (for Barrow and Leeds). Before this, Furness trains used the present platform 1 in both directions whilst Midland trains terminated in a bay behind what is now an ugly steel fence. As often as not, we are held in Carnforth platform waiting for traffic to pass on the main line before we can get the signal to venture out for our six mile run to Lancaster. At this stage, I find it impossible not to recall that by the direct route from Wennington, we would by now have passed Lancaster and perhaps already be in Morecambe.

Our train easily reaches its 70mph maximum on this stretch of the West Coast Main Line which, at Hest Bank, catches its one brief glimpse of the sea. There used to be a small fleet of camping coaches here. Hest Bank used to be a favourite place for people watching trains. I can remember, around 1960, the 'Pacifics' on Anglo-Scottish expresses, the Metro-Vic Co-Bos on the Lancaster–Barrow locals and the occasional train down the Morecambe branch collecting the single line token to Bare Lane from the signalman in the flat roof box which had replaced an earlier structure in 1958. The signal box is still there serving as just a level crossing frame.

After 1966, our Leeds–Morecambe train would have taken the branch from here into Morecambe thus completing the journey in perhaps only 10 minutes more than by the direct route. However, during the 1980s, they noticed the really big blunder of the 1966 diversion. The train missed Lancaster – far and away the largest traffic centre along the route – not just in its own right but for its connectional opportunities with the West Coast Main Line. You could no longer connect at Carnforth

'Standard' 4-6-0 No. 75042, with painted numerals in place of stolen number plate, passing Carnforth with empty tanks for Heysham on 31 July 1967. *(Tom Heavyside)*

so you had to change first at Carnforth or Bare Lane to reach Lancaster then make a second change. If travelling north, you would eventually go back through Carnforth. Since 1982, some, and then all, Leeds– Morecambe trains have therefore gone via Lancaster and not over the Hest Bank to Bare Lane spur. So, for the moment, Morecambe passengers will have to make do with a distant view of their destination as we head south to Lancaster.

We cross the River Lune just north of Lancaster Station. There is a pedestrian right of way over the viaduct. To the left we can see the former Midland Railway Viaduct, also crossing the Lune but now carrying road traffic. To the right, we see the old Midland formation, now a footpath and cycleway, disappearing towards Morecambe. Again we have to block the West Coast Main Line in both directions as we cross over to reach platform 2, one of the down bays, at Lancaster Castle, a station quite rich in history. The facade on the northbound side includes the original offices of the Lancaster & Carlisle Railway. It is, unfortunately, less convenient for the city centre than was the erstwhile Green Ayre Station.

We are booked to stand at Lancaster from 12.05 until 12.09. At the latter time, our signal has still not cleared – but we soon know why. A class 150dmu draws alongside us in the main line platform 3. It is going from Liverpool Lime Street to Morecambe. It should have left Lancaster at 11.55 and is 15 minutes late. As soon as it has gone, our signal clears and we set off in pursuit, one block section behind.

We are now travelling back along the West Coast Main Line towards Carnforth but at Morecambe South Junction we curve to the left on single track. Soon we are joined by another single line curving in from Hest Bank. The two fuse into one then immediately split again into what appears to be conventional double track. However each track from here to Morecambe is bi-directional. We take the right hand track and call at Bare Lane Station. This track leads to Morecambe Station and is controlled from Bare Lane box without token on the principle that no other train can enter this section until the previous one has been to Morecambe and back. What about the class 150 from Liverpool? That will have taken the left hand track which runs parallel with ours into Morecambe Station but with the difference that it has access to the Heysham branch which ours doesn't. The driver of the 150 will have collected a single line token from the Bare Lane signalman which could be used, though on this occasion it will not, to unlock the junction with the Heysham branch. We are only a minute or so behind our 12.21 arrival time when we finally trundle into Morecambe Station. On the other side of the island platform, the 150 is setting off back to Lancaster, slightly late, as the 12.15.

This is the 1994 Morecambe Station with rather basic facilities built near the site of the pre 1907 Northumberland Street. We are about 1/4 mile short of Promenade Station. The line was shortened in 1994 to make way for road improvements. We negotiate our way across this new road network built over the site of the platforms and sidings at Promenade Station finally reaching the main building which had been preserved as a restaurant. There we retire for lunch.

Despite the poor weather forecast, we emerge from lunch into the sunshine which has so far accompanied us all the way from home. We take a rather bracing walk along the promenade southward and back. The weather is still holding. Rather than potter round Morecambe until the train at 16.45, we decide to return by the Midland route. We set off from Morecambe Promenade for Lancaster Castle, calling at Scale Hall and Lancaster Green Ayre. Unfortunately the last electric train left just over 33 years ago so our only rolling stock is Adrian's 0-4-0 push chair.

The new Morecambe Station on 26 September 1995. 150137 on the 13.30 to Lancaster in platform 1. 142048 on the 13.35 to Heysham. *(F.W. Smith)*

Building the railway

First a few words about the two lines which the 'Little' North Western was intended to connect.

The Leeds & Bradford Railway

Incorporated in July 1844, and executed very quickly, the main line was opened on 30 June 1846 from Leeds Wellington to a terminus close to the present Bradford Forster Square.

Already, powers had been obtained in 1845 for an extension from Shipley, through the Aire Valley to Skipton and on to Colne. Work on this was carried out with equal speed permitting opening to Keighley on 16 March 1847, to Skipton on 7 September the same year and to Colne on 2 October 1848.

The Leeds & Bradford was taken over by the Midland Railway on the day it opened.

The Lancaster & Carlisle Railway

Simultaneously with work on the Leeds & Bradford, much larger 'armies' of navvies were toiling, some of them in far harder conditions, on the 69 miles between Lancaster and Carlisle. Authorised in June 1844, this line was built with incredible speed, opening as far north as Oxenholme on 23 September 1846 and through to Carlisle the following 17 December.

The Lancaster & Carlisle Railway was part of what has always been known as the West Coast Main Line, though it actually catches just the briefest glimpse of the sea at Hest Bank, near Morecambe.

The Lancaster & Carlisle was financed in part by the four companies – The London & Birmingham, Grand Junction, North Union and Preston & Lancaster Junction – which had collectively brought the railway from London as far as Lancaster. These companies amalgamated in 1846 to form the London & North Western Railway. The Lancaster & Carlisle remained independent but was worked by the LNWR from its opening until August 1857 when it assumed responsibility for its own operation. This lasted only two years when the LNWR took it over for fear that it might fall into the hands of the Midland Railway.

Skipton old station, in use from 1847 until 1876, about ½ mile east of the present structure. *(Peter E. Baughan)*

The facade of Lancaster Castle Station, northbound side, which incorporates the original offices of the Lancaster & Carlisle Railway. *(Martin Bairstow)*

Skipton Station 1936. Ex L&Y 2-4-2T No. 10795 is on the train of empty coaches. Another ex L&Y 'radial' tank stands at platform 5 on the Ilkley line. *(D. Ibbotson Collection)*

Black Five No 45273 at Skipton with a Heysham to Leeds parcels in June 1967. *(Jim Davenport)*

The 'Little' North Western Railway

By 1845 it was clear that there would soon be a railway at Skipton and also one between Lancaster and Carlisle. This left a gap of about 40 miles which, if filled, would offer a continuous railway from the Midlands and West Riding to Carlisle and Scotland.

Such was the pace of railway promotion – 1845 was the peak year of the 'Mania' – that a number of schemes were put forward to link Skipton with the West Coast Main Line. The only one to make any progress was the North Western Railway.

In February 1845, a Provisional Committee issued a prospectus for a main line connecting the Leeds & Bradford just north of Skipton with the Lancaster & Carlisle at Low Gill. There was to be a branch from Clapham to Lancaster. It was also proposed to build a branch from Kirkby Lonsdale to join the West Coast Main Line by a triangular junction north of Milnthorpe. This last idea was to have been associated with a railway from Milnthorpe to Ulverston and Barrow which failed to get Parliamentary approval. The proposed North Western branch to Milnthorpe was also rejected.

The remainder of the North Western Railway from Skipton to Low Gill with the branch to Lancaster, was authorised by Act of Parliament on 26 June 1846.

Construction was formally inaugurated on New Year's Eve 1846 with the then fashionable ceremony of cutting the first sod. The ritual was enacted close to what we now know as Settle Junction where the main road, then the Keighley and Kendal Turnpike, is adjacent. Lord Morpeth, MP for the West Riding, succeeded in amusing his audience by dressing as a navvy but struggled to fill the mahogany barrow because the ground he was supposed to be digging was frozen hard. Amongst the guests were George Hudson of the Midland and Edmund Dennison of the Great Northern Railway – an indication perhaps of the importance with which the project was viewed.

The task of building the railway was entrusted to a number of contractors. Millar and Nelson bid successfully in January 1847 for the Settle to Clapham contract. Other sections were awarded over the following months.

The Morecambe Harbour & Railway Company

This enterprise was promoted to build harbour works at Morecambe together with three miles of railway track to link with the 'Little' North Western at Lancaster Green Ayre. The so called William Lands branch was also proposed to give access to the Lancaster & Carlisle Railway near Hest Bank.

The project came before Parliament in the same 1845-46 session as the North Western Bill. It was in danger of foundering for want of credible financial backing. In its own interests, the North Western Railway supported the Morecambe Company which secured its Act of Parliament on 16 July 1846. Immediately afterwards, the two companies amalgamated.

A Metro Cammel dmu on Morecambe to Leeds service pulling away from Gargrave in February 1987.
(Alan Young)

75059 passing Gargrave southbound with tankers probably from Heysham. The empty coal wagons are to provide space between the loco firebox and the loaded tanks. *(David Beeken)*

70053 'Moray Firth' passing the low platforms at Bell Busk with the southbound 'Waverley' in May 1959, the month the station closed. *(Peter Sunderland)*

Lancaster to Morecambe became the first section of the 'Little' North Western Railway to be completed. After an inspection by Captain Wynne of the Board of Trade, it opened on Whit Monday 12 June 1848 with a dozen trains each way and four on Sundays. The track was single.

The William Lands branch was never built. Instead, the 'Little' North Western obtained powers in May 1849 for a short line diagonally opposite connecting Green Ayre with the Lancaster & Carlisle Railway at Castle Station. This opened on 18 December 1849 and always remained single track.

Progress on the Main Line

The 'Little' North Western Railway had been promoted in 1845/46 at the height of the 'Railway Mania'. Almost immediately, the trade cycle had moved into recession making it hard to raise capital or even to collect calls on shares to which shareholders were contractually bound. In February 1848, the Company turned for advice to George Stephenson. He recommended that they should devote available resources into completing a single line from Skipton to Lancaster, including connection with the Lancaster & Carlisle Railway but should suspend work on the route to Low Gill.

Between Clapham and Ingleton, work was so advanced that it was decided to complete this section. North of Ingleton, however, work was stopped and the contractor was moved onto the Lancaster line.

The route from Skipton to Ingleton opened on 31 July 1849. Lancaster Green Ayre to Wennington followed in November 1849. The gap between Wennington and Clapham was covered by a horse bus for the next six months. Wennington to Bentham opened on 2 May 1850 to be followed only a month later by the remaining Bentham to Clapham section on 1 June.

At first, the entire route from Skipton to Morecambe was single line but the second track was in use by late 1850 all the way from Hellifield to Hornby. During the next three years, the track was doubled between Skipton and Hellifield. It was not until 1877 that the Lancaster to Morecambe section was doubled. Hornby to Lancaster was not widened until 1889.

In anticipation of the Skipton to Ingleton opening, the 'Little' North Western tried to arrange for the Midland Railway to work the daily service of four passenger trains each way. Negotiations failed to produce an agreement so the 'Little' North Western resolved to manage on their own.

They subcontracted the operation to Edmund Sharpe who had been a founder director of both the 'Little' North Western and the Morecambe Harbour & Railway Company. He had also been the first secretary of the 'Little' North Western. He had

LMS 4F 0-6-0 No. 44345 heading coke hoppers south through Long Preston on 17 March 1962.
(P. B. Booth/N. E. Stead Collection)

Long Preston Station buildings, looking north on 3 September 1964. *(Peter E. Baughan)*

Caprotti Black Five 4-6-0 No. 44753 speeding south through Long Preston with a fitted freight on 17 March 1962. *(P. B. Booth/N. E. Stead Collection)*

vacated these offices in order to become the Company's supplier of locomotives and rolling stock for which purpose he leased workshop premises from the 'Little' North Western Railway at Lancaster.

Sharpe produced a motley collection of rolling stock including passenger carriages which were both short and wide, dangerously close to exceeding the loading gauge. At the end of 1850, he had 11 locomotives in traffic, all of them named:

0-4-0	'Hornby Castle'
0-4-0	'Skipton Castle'
0-4-0	'Lancaster Castle'
2-2-2T	'Whernside'
2-2-2T	'Pennighent'
0-2-2T	'Saddleback'
0-2-2T	'Skiddaw'
0-2-2T	'Black Comb'
0-2-2T	'Helvellyn'
0-2-2T	'Ingleborough'
0-2-2T	'Clougha'

The first five engines had been built new by Sharpe. The other six were up to nine years old.

The arrangement with Sharpe did not last long. From 1 June 1852, the 'Little' North Western Railway was worked by the Midland – effectively making it a part of the Midland Railway although it was not fully absorbed until 1871. Until then, the local Company remained as landlord, occasionally seeking to get the Low Gill line moving.

Assets handed over to the Midland in 1852 included 12 locomotives, 17 passenger carriages, eight new coke wagons, two old vans, an old horse box, eight old wagons and an engine 'in course of alteration', plus sundry stores, horses and harness.

Edmund Sharpe was redundant but in 1854 he turned up on the Liverpool, Crosby & Southport Railway which was assuming operation of its own line. Evidently his experience with the 'Little' North Western was thought to be what they needed.

Bradshaw for November 1850 shows four trains each way. The first at 7.30 from Lancaster Green Ayre is the 'Government' train carrying third class passengers at 1d. per mile. It calls at all stations. The other three trains are first and second class only starting from Lancaster Castle at 11.15am, 3.40 and 7.30pm. The 3.40 is the 'express' calling only at Green Ayre, Caton, Hornby, Bentham, Settle and Gargrave. It commands a slightly higher fare in both classes. The two Sunday trains are first, second and third class.

The Morecambe line is worked separately with five trains each way (three on Sunday) not connecting particularly well for Skipton. This is before the harbour was open at Morecambe.

The 1860 timetable shows five trains each way on the main line, all but one apparently serving both Morecambe and Lancaster Castle. Whether by through carriage or connection at Green Ayre is unclear but the Belfast 'Boat Trains' were certainly through to Morecambe. There were some additional trains between Green Ayre and Morecambe. All trains on that section were advertised as 'Gov' carrying third class passengers as well as first and second.

4F 0-6-0 No. 44468 negotiating Clapham Junction from the Wennington line on 27 September 1959.
(Martin Bairstow Collection)

Bentham Station looking towards Skipton about 1910. The 'Little' North Western main building here was replaced in the 1950s. *(Peter E. Baughan)*

LMS 'Crab' 2-6-0 No. 42928 arriving at Bentham with a Morecambe to Leeds semi fast on 17 March 1962. *(P. B. Booth/N. E. Stead Collection)*

Patriot Class 4-6-0 No. 45510 entering Wennington from Morecambe on 5 March 1962. The loco will detatch, then pick up the Carnforth portion from the bay on the right before taking the combined train on to Leeds. *(D. Butterfield/N. E. Stead Collection)*

Ivatt Class 4 No. 43039 entering Wennington with a Morecambe to Leeds stopper in 1958. The container on the leading flat wagon could well be on a household removal service. *(Peter Sunderland)*

Caton looking towards Lancaster in Midland days. *(Alan Young Collection)*

A Leeds bound 'Black Five' crossing the River Lune by the easternmost of the Crook O' Lune viaducts. *(P.L. Greenall, courtesy David Beeken)*

Halton Station viewed from a Leeds to Morecambe train in September 1963. The village is at the other side of the river. The station building is a replacement for the original wooden structure which was destroyed by fire on 3 April 1907. Sparks from the Heysham to St. Pancras 'Boat Train' ignited inflammable material in the goods yard.
(Peter E. Baughan)

The bridge giving access from Halton village to the station. The structure was rebuilt in 1911 using materials recovered from the Old Lune Viaduct or Greyhound Bridge at Lancaster. Until closure of Halton Station in 1966, there was a toll for vehicles using the bridge.
(Martin Bairstow)

Lancaster Green Ayre is seen on 28 December 1965, a few days before closure. The right hand vehicle is a post war LMS 'port hole' coach.
(Geoffrey Lewthwaite)

Ingleton to Low Gill

D27 passing Ingleton with the northbound 'Thames – Clyde Express', diverted off the Settle & Carlisle Line on 9 September 1961. *(P. B. Booth/N. E. Stead Collection)*

On 1 June 1850, the 'Little' North Western Railway was complete between Skipton, Lancaster and Morecambe. At that stage, prospects for the original main line to Low Gill were so bleak that the company closed the Clapham to Ingleton section which had been in operation for just ten months. The Ingleton line was to remain closed for the next 11 years whilst the 'Little' North Western and neighbouring railway companies argued about filling the gap to Low Gill.

The fundamental problem was that the 'Little' North Western could not raise the capital so they looked for a partner or backer. An obvious candidate was the Midland Railway but in the early 1850s, that company was part of the 'Euston Square Confederacy', a secret cartel arrangement with the London & North Western Railway. The LNWR did not want, and the Midland did not need the alternative route to Scotland which completion of the 'Little' North Western would achieve.

A prime objective of the 'Euston Square Confederacy' had been to strangle the Great Northern Railway which, by 1849, was operating an almost direct route from London to Leeds, a strong threat to the earlier LNWR/Midland route via Rugby and Derby. If the GNR could secure running powers over the Midland from Leeds to Skipton, the 'Little' North Western to Low Gill and over the Lancaster & Carlisle, then it would have an Anglo-Scottish route to rival that of the 'Confederates'. The possibility of the GNR reaching Carlisle was taken sufficiently seriously for the LNWR and Midland to make concessions to the GNR over the allocation of revenues and, for the time being at least, the GNR abandoned its interest in getting to Carlisle.

The main feeder to the Lancaster & Carlisle Railway was the LNWR. Completion of the Ingleton–Low Gill section would provide alternative access from the south either by the Midland, which was in league with the LNWR, or by the Great Northern which would have to bridge the gap from Leeds to Skipton – presumably by running powers over the Midland.

Having failed to get either the Midland or the Great Northern to finance the Low Gill line, the 'Little' North Western tried the Lancaster & Carlisle. This company was under strong influence from the LNWR but occasionally tried to flex its own muscles. The Ingleton route would give it greater independence.

The 'Little' North Western proposed that the Ingleton–Low Gill section be built jointly with the Lancaster & Carlisle. However, a majority of Lancaster & Carlisle directors preferred to keep in with the LNWR and the scheme failed.

In 1855, the 'Little' North Western decided to go it alone by promoting a new Bill to revive earlier powers which had expired for building the Ingleton to Low Gill line. It also sought extensive running rights over neighbouring lines including the Great Northern, Midland, Lancaster & Carlisle and two Scottish companies.

The main part of the Bill was successful but the running powers were defeated by the opposition of the companies over whose lines they were sought. The Bill was withdrawn but not before it had broken the 'Euston Square Confederacy' by bringing to public notice, the illegal cartel which was being practised.

The Midland Railway then began to distance itself from the LNWR. Instead it was moving closer to the Great Northern into whose London terminus at Kings Cross, it was going to transfer its business away from Euston once its Bedford to Hitchin line was built.

In approving part of the 'Little' North Western's 1855 Bill, Parliament had accepted that completion of the Ingleton route was in the public interest. If another Bill was introduced, especially without the disputed running powers, then it was likely to be passed.

The Lancaster & Carlisle Railway had spent a lot of money opposing the 'Little' North Western's Bill. It began to wonder if a better use of resources would not be to build the line itself.

In 1857, two Bills came before Parliament, both seeking powers for essentially the same thing. A House of Commons Committee had to decide between the proposals of the 'Little' North Western and the Lancaster & Carlisle. They found in favour of the latter who were obliged, under the resultant Act, to purchase from the 'Little' North Western, all the land and part completed works which had stood idle since 1849.

At first The Midland Railway appeared satisfied with this outcome. The Ingleton–Low Gill line was going to be built at no expense to them. The Lancaster & Carlisle was in a far better position than the 'Little' North Western actually to complete the work. Had Parliament favoured the 'Little' North Western, the Midland might have ended up having to finance it.

The first thing the Lancaster & Carlisle did was to seek an amending Act to water down the scheme by cutting out the south facing junction near Low Gill and by sharpening the north facing curve thereby creating anything but a high speed junction. The 'Little' North Western was successful in persuading Parliament to modify the severity of the curve. This obliged the Lancaster & Carlisle to build the 11 arch viaduct across the Dillicar Beck rather than lay the line along the valley side. In addition, Low Gill station had to be resited because the existing station was too far south of the junction. Work was divided into four contracts which were let during 1858. The largest works were the viaducts at Low Gill, Sedbergh and Ingleton.

48756 with a northbound freight at Ingleton on 9 September 1961. *(P. B. Booth/N. E. Stead Collection)*

Sedbergh Station looking North about 1920.
(Peter E. Baughan Collection)

Fowler 2-6-4T No. 42396 pauses at Kirkby Lonsdale with a Clapham to Low Gill on 26 September 1953.
(B. G. Tweed/N. E. Stead Collection)

Barbon looking north on 13 April 1955. The level crossing was the only one on the Clapham to Low Gill line.
(F. W. Shuttleworth)

The Leeds bound platform at Clapham junction for Ingleton about 1915.
(Peter E. Baughan Collection)

Opening of the 'Ingleton Branch'

The Ingleton to Low Gill line opened in 1861, to goods on 24 August and to passengers on 16 September. To the LNWR, it was officially known as the 'Ingleton Branch'. Initially, just two passenger trains were operated each weekday. At the Low Gill end, they ran through to Tebay where better connections were available. But at the southern end, they terminated at the LNWR's own Ingleton Station, known locally as Thornton, which was situated just to the north of Ingleton Viaduct.

On 1 October 1861, the Midland Railway reopened the Clapham to Ingleton line which it had widened to double track. Shortly afterwards, it replaced the temporary 1849 station at Ingleton with a permanent one.

Despite this, the LNWR continued to terminate on the other side of the viaduct. Stories of passengers struggling across town with lots of luggage may be slightly exaggerated. They may even have been Midland propaganda. By 1862 some LNWR trains were running into the Midland station. Better connections and through carriages were introduced.

None the less, the Midland remained dissatisfied and began threatening to build an independent route to Carlisle. The LNWR responded by proposing that the Midland share its lease over the Lancaster & Carlisle Railway thereby creating a joint line from Ingleton to Carlisle.

Negotiations seem to have broken down over one issue. The Midland wanted freedom to fix its own fares and charges independent of the LNWR. The latter company agreed to this except for traffic stopping intermediately at stations on the Lancaster & Carlisle. This may have been agreeable to the Midland had they not included Carlisle itself on the list of L&C stations. The Midland claimed that all their traffic would stop at Carlisle so this clause was not just protecting LNWR local traffic. It was imposing LNWR control over all Midland fares and charges. Instead the Midland went ahead with its Bill seeking powers to build the Settle & Carlisle line.

Condemned to Remain a Branch

When presenting its Settle & Carlisle Bill, the Midland Railway had to persuade both Houses of Parliament that the public interest would be served by its proposed independent route to Scotland. It was supported by other railway companies who wanted to overcome the monopoly of the London & North Western Railway. Strong support came from the Glasgow & South Western and the North British who would take traffic from Carlisle onto Glasgow and Edinburgh and from the Lancashire & Yorkshire Railway who hoped to feed Liverpool and Manchester traffic into the Midland at Hellifield.

The most vociferous opponent of the scheme was the London & North Western Railway who argued that the Ingleton route already served the public interest quite adequately. Parliament was not persuaded to protect the monopoly of the LNWR so on 16 July 1866, the Midland Railway (Settle & Carlisle) Bill became an Act.

Before work had got seriously started, the Midland and LNWR made another attempt at compromise. One company was faced with the massive task of building the 71 mile Settle & Carlisle line. The other would have to meet the high cost of leasing the Lancaster & Carlisle line on its own. A compromise was reached in November 1868 for a joint lease without any of the falling out over fares and charges which had defeated earlier negotiations. Part of the settlement was that the Midland Railway should apply to Parliament for abandonment of its Settle & Carlisle powers.

A Bill to this effect was argued before a Parliamentary Committee in April 1869. This time the LNWR was on the Midland side. However, the

Top:
Waterside viaduct, north of Sedbergh in 1955.
(F.W. Shuttleworth)

Opposite:
Ingleton looking north over the viaduct on 22 June 1964. The thrice weekly branch goods has only a light payload. *(Peter E. Baughan)*

Below:
Kirkby Lonsdale looking north on 13 April, 1955. 42393 on the branch goods is visible in the yard. *(F.W. Shuttleworth)*

Fowler 2-6-4T No. 42396 on arrival at Low Gill from Clapham on 26 September 1953.
(B. G. Tweed/N. E. Stead Collection)

Companies who had supported the previous Settle & Carlisle Bill felt they had been used by the Midland as a lever against the LNWR. So did Parliament and the Abandonment Bill was rejected.

This meant that the Midland Railway was compelled to carry out the works authorised by the 1866 Act. Of course, if they had failed in the task, the Settle & Carlisle would not have been built. But the Midland would have lost face and would have remained at the mercy of the LNWR because the joint lease of the Lancaster & Carlisle had also been rejected as part of the Abandonment Bill.

There was no question of the Midland Railway not taking up the task. The Settle & Carlisle line was completed in a creditable seven years from the defeat of the Abandonment Bill. It opened throughout for goods on 2 August 1875 and passengers on 1 May 1876. The Midland had its route to Scotland but it wasn't via Ingleton which continued to be served by two branch lines meeting end on. One from Clapham and the other from Low Gill.

A Quiet Backwater

For the best part of a century, the Ingleton branch pottered on, never to realise the potential for which it had supposedly been built.

Bradshaw for April 1910 shows four weekday trains leaving Tebay for Ingleton at 7.34 and 10.20am, 4.25 and 7.05pm. All but the last one go through to the Midland station where connections on to Clapham require waits of 12 minutes, 37 minutes and 1 hour 26 minutes. That was only to Clapham where a further change was required to get any further.

The Midland ran five trains each way between Ingleton and Clapham, timed as far as possible to connect both for Skipton and for Lancaster. There were two extras on a Saturday but no service on this or the LNWR branch on a Sunday.

Something of a revolution took place from 1 July 1910 when the Midland introduced its 'Lake District Express'. This left London St Pancras at 5am calling at Leicester, Nottingham and Sheffield. From Leeds it ran non stop via Ingleton to Penrith where connections were available for Keswick and Cockermouth. The train then went on to Carlisle and Edinburgh. In the other direction the train left Edinburgh Waverley at 10.30am, reaching St Pancras at 7.15pm.

Relations between railway companies had matured considerably by this time. It had taken 49 years since the Ingleton branch opened and was only one train in the peak summer season. Emergency diversions apart, this was the one instance of the Ingleton branch being used as a main line. It lasted only until the outbreak of the First World War.

Ingleton (LNWR) station closed on the last day of

1916, part of a nationwide 'temporary' closure of insignificant stations to free staff for slaughter on the Western Front. It never reopened to passengers but the adjacent coalyard remained in business until 1965.

From 1 January 1923, the Midland and LNWR were both part of the London Midland & Scottish Railway. Ingleton was no longer a 'frontier' station.

The LMS timetable for early summer 1934 shows no radical change from the times quoted although two trains do run through to Clapham. Departures from Tebay are at 7.54 and 9.10am, both to Clapham and at 1.50 and 5.51pm only as far as Ingleton. There are nine trains in total from Ingleton to Clapham with an extra late service on Thursdays and Saturdays only. There are no Sunday trains apart from a rather strange unbalanced working at 4.15pm from Kirkby Lonsdale to Tebay. This does not appear in the peak summer timetable for 1938 when the only Sunday train is a 3.28pm Clapham to Ingleton and 7.45pm the other way. There is one long distance train shown in the July 1938 timetable: A Fridays and Saturdays only train each way between Leeds and Keswick which has stops on the branch at Clapham, Ingleton, Kirkby Lonsdale and Sedbergh.

Decline and Closure

The Second World War saw a curtailment of the ordinary service. *Bradshaw* for November 1944 shows only two trains per day from Tebay at 9.10am to Clapham and 7.35pm to Ingleton. There are four trains shown between Ingleton and Clapham at 7.14 and 10.02am, 12.55 and 5.00pm. There was, however, some special traffic including petrol to a depot near Sedbergh.

The timetable was improved after the War. In 1953 there were four trains on the former LNWR section and six on the Midland with the customary Saturday evening extra from Ingleton to Clapham and back.

The route was closed to ordinary traffic on 30 January 1954. Fowler 2-6-4T No.42396 worked the 6.42pm Clapham to Tebay, the 8.30pm back to Ingleton and then the 9.45 Saturdays only to Clapham and return. 42396 was the last engine based at Ingleton Shed which was not required after withdrawal of the passenger service.

There remained the occasional ramblers' excursion. In addition, special trains continued to run at the beginning and end of terms for benefit of boarding schools at Sedbergh, Barbon (for

'Compound' 4-4-0 No. 41102 approaching Low Gill with a northbound special, 1950s.
(N. E. Stead Collection)

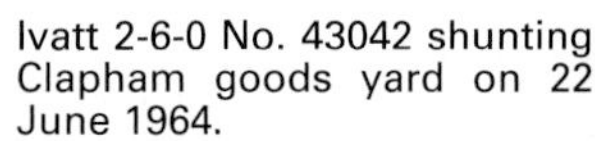

Ivatt 2-6-0 No. 43042 shunting Clapham goods yard on 22 June 1964.
(Peter E. Baughan)

Casterton School) and Kirkby Lonsdale. The practice lasted until the early 1960s by which time the line saw only a thrice weekly pick up goods. Barbon closed to goods at the end of February 1964. Sedbergh and Kirkby Lonsdale followed at the end of September leaving only the two Ingleton Yards (ex Midland and LNWR) which were served from Clapham direction until the end of February 1965. After this date, there was no regular traffic but the line continued to be maintained as a possible emergency diversionary route until official closure on 26 July 1966.

An Opportunity Wasted?

The Beeching Report of March 1963 recommended closure of the Settle & Carlisle line. That route would never have been built had railway politics of the 1860s not forced the Midland to go for an independent route in order to overcome its frustrations at Ingleton. Intermediate traffic on the Settle & Carlisle was always secondary to its role as a through route. If British Railways had really been concerned at the cost of maintaining the 71 mile Settle & Carlisle line, they could easily have diverted through traffic via Ingleton thus having to maintain only 23 self contained route miles with fewer large engineering works.

By keeping the Ingleton line open until 1966, even after it had ceased to carry traffic, they may have been allowing for this long term possibility and not just insuring against snowdrifts on the Settle & Carlisle. In closing, and then immediately destroying the Ingleton line, they threw away the alternative to the Settle & Carlisle. At that time, closures were a main thrust of railway policy. One can only conclude that they were so confident of severing all railway communication between Leeds and Carlisle that they saw no need to retain the option of the cheaper, and possibly more productive, alternative.

In the 1980s, the threatened Settle & Carlisle closure became a 'cause célèbre' – an eight year marathon which resulted in the line getting a new lease of life. The point is now totally academic but one can't help wonder if it would have been better for Leeds–Carlisle trains to go via Ingleton, serving Penrith which is a larger town than all places between Settle and Carlisle put together. If the route mileage saved (71 less 23) had gone into keeping open feeder lines such as Penrith to Keswick, then the present day network would be more effective.

The track was lifted during 1967. After that parts of the route gradually returned to other uses. Bridges were removed, sections of embankment swept away to allow road widening.

There is nothing to see at Barbon where a housing estate has been built on the station site. Middleton on Lune is the only station still standing, a remote spot alongside the Kirkby Lonsdale to Sedbergh road.

The principal memorials to this lost route to Scotland are the viaducts. Ingleton with its 11 arches of white sandstone still spans the Greta Gorge. Just south of Sedbergh, a single steel arch spans the River Rawthey at an acute angle. It is supported on either side of the river by red sandstone parapets.

North of Sedbergh, the River Lune is crossed by Waterside Viaduct. This comprises a steel centre span, very similar to that over the Rawthey but here it is supported on either side by three arches in red sandstone. It can easily be viewed from the Sedbergh to Low Gill road. The northernmost monument is the eleven arch curving viaduct at Low Gill. Also built in red sandstone, it spans the Dillicar Beck. It can be viewed both from the adjacent road and, briefly, from passing trains on the West Coast Main Line.

Sedbergh looking north on 16 January 1954. *(F. W. Shuttleworth)*

8F 2-8-0 No. 48756 with a northbound freight, diverted off the Settle & Carlisle line in August 1961. It has just crossed Low Gill Viaduct, obscured by the exhaust, and is approaching Low Gill itself.
(Peter Sunderland)

4-6-0 No. 46102 'Black Watch' passing Low Gill on the main line with a southbound express in April 1960.
(Peter Sunderland)

D 1495

SUNDAYS, June 7th and 28th and
*** WEDNESDAY, June 17th, 1931**

(* Restaurant Car Train)

Cook's HALF-DAY EXCURSIONS to

CLAPHAM, INGLETON §KIRKBY LONSDALE SEDBERGH & KESWICK

FROM	Times of Departure.		RETURN FARES (Third Class) TO				
	June 7th and 28th.	June 17th.	Clapham.	Ingleton.	§ Kirkby Lonsdale.	Sedbergh.	Keswick.
	a.m.	a.m.	s. d.	s. d.	s. d.	s. d.	s. d.
LEEDS (Wellington)	10 0	11 25	3 6	4 0	4 0	4 6	6 6
		p.m.					
KEIGHLEY	10 25	12 1	2 6	3 0	3 0	3 6	5 6
SKIPTON	10 40	12 20	2 0	2 6	2 6	3 0	5 0
Arrive (June 7th and 28th)...	—	—	a.m. 11 18	a.m. 11 28	a.m. 11 40	noon 12 0	p.m. 1 35
„ (June 17th)	—	—	p.m. 12 58	p.m. 1 10	—	p.m. 1 37	3 11

§—Bookings on June 7th and 28th only.

CHILDREN under three years of age, free; three years and under fourteen, half-fares.

JUNE 17th ONLY.
MEALS-EN-ROUTE HOT LUNCHEON and HOT SUPPER, 5s. for the two meals, will be served on the forward and return journeys respectively.

Tickets for meals must be obtained in advance at the L M S Stations, or at Messrs. Cook's Office, 55, Boar Lane, Leeds.

RESTAURANT ACCOMMODATION STRICTLY LIMITED.

RESERVATION OF SEATS.—Seats may be reserved at the principal stations (with certain exceptions) for passengers joining trains at the starting points.—Reservation fee, 1/- per seat.

RETURN ARRANGEMENTS.—Passengers return same day as under :—

		June 7th and 28th.	June 17th.
KESWICK	dep.	6 5 p.m.	7 30 p.m.
SEDBERGH	„	7 55 „	9 20 „
KIRKBY LONSDALE	„	8 15 „	—
INGLETON	„	8 25 „	9 42 „
CLAPHAM	„	8 38 „	9 53 „

For particulars of CHEAP HOLIDAY RETURN TICKETS issued on Fridays and Saturdays to all parts, and daily between certain places, see separate announcements.

CONDITIONS OF ISSUE OF EXCURSION TICKETS AND OTHER REDUCED FARE TICKETS.
Excursion tickets and tickets issued at fares less than the ordinary fares are issued subject to the Notices and Conditions shown in the Company's Current Time Tables.

Passengers holding day or half-day excursion tickets by special trains are not allowed to take any luggage except small handbags, luncheon baskets, or other small articles intended for the passenger's use during the day. On the return journey only, passengers may take with them, free of charge at Owner's Risk, goods for their own use not exceeding 60 lbs.

Passengers are requested to obtain their Tickets in advance, as this will assist the Company in the provision of accommodation.

TICKETS CAN BE PURCHASED at the COMPANY'S STATIONS and BOOKING OFFICES ; at the Offices of THOS. COOK & SON, LTD., 55, Boar Lane, LEEDS ; Messrs. A. ALTHAM, LTD., 4, New Market Street, 255, Hunslet Road, and 34a, Tong Road, LEEDS ; TRAVELLERS, LTD., 5, Boar Lane, LEEDS ; and at Messrs. A. ALTHAM, LTD., 22, Low Street, KEIGHLEY, and Winterwell Buildings, Swadford Street, SKIPTON.

PLEASE RETAIN THIS BILL FOR REFERENCE.

H 218/R

WHITSUNTIDE, 1934

Whit-Monday, May 21st

Special Half-Day Excursion

TO

MORECAMBE

(PROMENADE)

FROM	Times of Departure.	RETURN FARES, Third Class.
	p.m.	s. d.
Tebay	1 30	3 0 (Tebay to Kirkby Lonsdale)
Low Gill...	1 35	
Sedbergh	1 50	
Barbon	2 0	
Kirkby Lonsdale	2 10	
Ingleton	2 25	2 6
Clapham...	2 35	2 0
Bentham...	2 50	1 6
Morecambe (Prom.) arrive	3 25	

RETURN ARRANGEMENTS.

Passengers return same day from Morecambe (Promenade) at 10-30 p.m.

(Passengers for all stations except Bentham and Clapham, change at Clapham, going forward by Special Train at **11-32 p.m.**)

Children above 3 and under 14 years of age, half-fares

Tickets, Bills and information can be obtained in advance at the Stations

Conditions of issue of Excursion Tickets and other Tickets at less than Ordinary Fare.
These Tickets are issued subject to the Notices and Conditions shown in the Company's current Time Tables. For Luggage Allowances also see Time Tables.

For further particulars apply to Mr. F. K. ROGERS, District Goods and Passenger Manager, Barrow-in-Furness.

May, 1934. (X5/Whit/34) **ASHTON DAVIES,**
(E.R.O. 53302) **Chief Commercial Manager.**

(25—1,000) Barrow Printing Co. Ltd., Lawson Street, Barrow-in-Furness. H 218/R

The Furness & Midland Joint

31448 takes the Leeds line, leaving Carnforth Station on 6 October 1984.
(Tom Heavyside)

In 1862 the Furness and Midland Railways agreed to build, at joint expense, a direct link between their two systems at Carnforth and Wennington. Upon completion, the line was to be operated by the Midland but maintained by the Furness who would staff the stations and signal boxes.

Despite opposition from the London & North Western Railway, the line gained authorisation in June 1863. From the Midland point of view, it promised direct access to the Furness area for freight, to the Lake District for passengers and to port facilities at Piel and Barrow which would allow for development of Irish traffic on a scale not possible at Morecambe.

For the Furness, the joint line offered a direct connection to a second main line company reducing dependence on the LNWR. For Iron ore travelling to the West Riding it would avoid use of the LNWR main line between Carnforth and Lancaster with reversal at Lancaster Castle. It would bypass the difficult gradient between Castle and Green Ayre and miss the remaining single line bottleneck between there and Hornby.

The line opened to goods on 10 April 1867 and to passengers on 6 June. At first, passenger trains terminated at a temporary station by what became Carnforth East Junction. However, from 1 July 1868, they were extended to a station at Carnforth F&M Junction where interchange was possible with the Furness Railway. For the next 12 years Furness trains stopped at two stations in Carnforth – one shared with the LNWR and one with the Midland. The station at F&M Junction closed in 1880 when the sharp curve opened from East Junction to the main Carnforth Station which was rebuilt to accommodate LNWR, Furness and Midland trains. There were two straight platforms on the LNWR main line with two tracks but only one platform curving away under an overall roof for the Furness line. Midland trains left from a bay by the north end of the Furness platform.

Direct trains from Leeds to Barrow missed the new Carnforth Station. On some workings, the Midland train from Leeds would stop before East Junction, to allow the Barrow coaches in the rear to be uncoupled before the Midland loco drew the front portion into Carnforth Station. A Furness engine would then back on to the rear portion and take it to Barrow.

The bay platform at Wennington faced Leeds confirming that the purpose was not to run a local service from Wennington to Carnforth. Even the all stations trains over the F&M were portions of through trains from Leeds. In the westbound direction, the combined train would draw into Wennington platform where the two portions would be uncoupled. The front coaches would go forward with the train engine, usually to Morecambe. The rear portion, usually for Carnforth, would then follow, typically four minutes later, with an engine which would have been waiting ahead, just beyond the junction.

In the reverse direction, the first train to arrive at Wennington, usually from Carnforth, would run through the station and set back into the bay platform. Its engine would disappear. The train from Morecambe would then arrive in the main platform. Its engine would uncouple and go collect the carriages in the bay which it would pull out and set back onto the rest of the train in the main platform, ready for departure towards Leeds.

This appears to have been the procedure according to a series of photographs taken by John Halliday in 1957. It is likely that other methods were used at different times between 1867 and 1966. The dividing and joining of diesel multiple units presented no problem but that practice lasted less than 12 months prior to diversion of the Morecambe trains.

An Ivatt 2-6-0 entering Wennington from Morecambe on 11 October 1958. It will detatch in the platform in order to collect the Carnforth portion from the bay. The Fowler tank which brought these three coaches is just visible under the road bridge. *(J.C.W. Halliday)*

Whilst the compound waits to set back onto its Leeds–Morecambe train, 40041 sets off with the Carnforth portion. Wennington Junction 1956. *(Peter Sunderland)*

Transition from steam to diesel. D5254 pilots 92128 on the Heysham to Teesside ammonia train approaching Wennington from Carnforth on 16 September 1967.
(Martin Bairstow Collection)

Midland 2-4-0 No. 209 emerging from Melling Tunnel, heading towards Carnforth in the early 1930s. The locomotive was over 50 years old and nearing the end of its life. *(D. Ibbotson)*

Ex Southern Railway 4-6-0 No. 850 'Lord Nelson' crossing the Keer Viaduct at Carpernwray, west of Borwick with the 'Cumbrian Mountain Express' to Hellifield on 4 April, 1981. *(Tom Heavyside)*

'Black Five' No. 44932, then painted green, taking the Leeds line at Carnforth with a special on 21 September 1974. *(Tom Heavyside)*

Carnforth East Junction, 1959. The train is going towards Barrow. The curve to Carnforth Station is on the left.
(Peter Sunderland)

The temporary station at Carnforth, used only from June 1867 to June 1868, still almost standing in 1959.
(Peter Sunderland)

'Black Five' No. 44680 entering Carnforth from the North on 31 July 1967.
(Tom Heavyside)

Carnforth Station looking north about 1905, Furness platform to the left, LNWR to the right.
(Peter E. Baughan Collection)

92012 pauses in Carnforth Station with a train of empty stock on 31 July 1967. *(Tom Heavyside)*

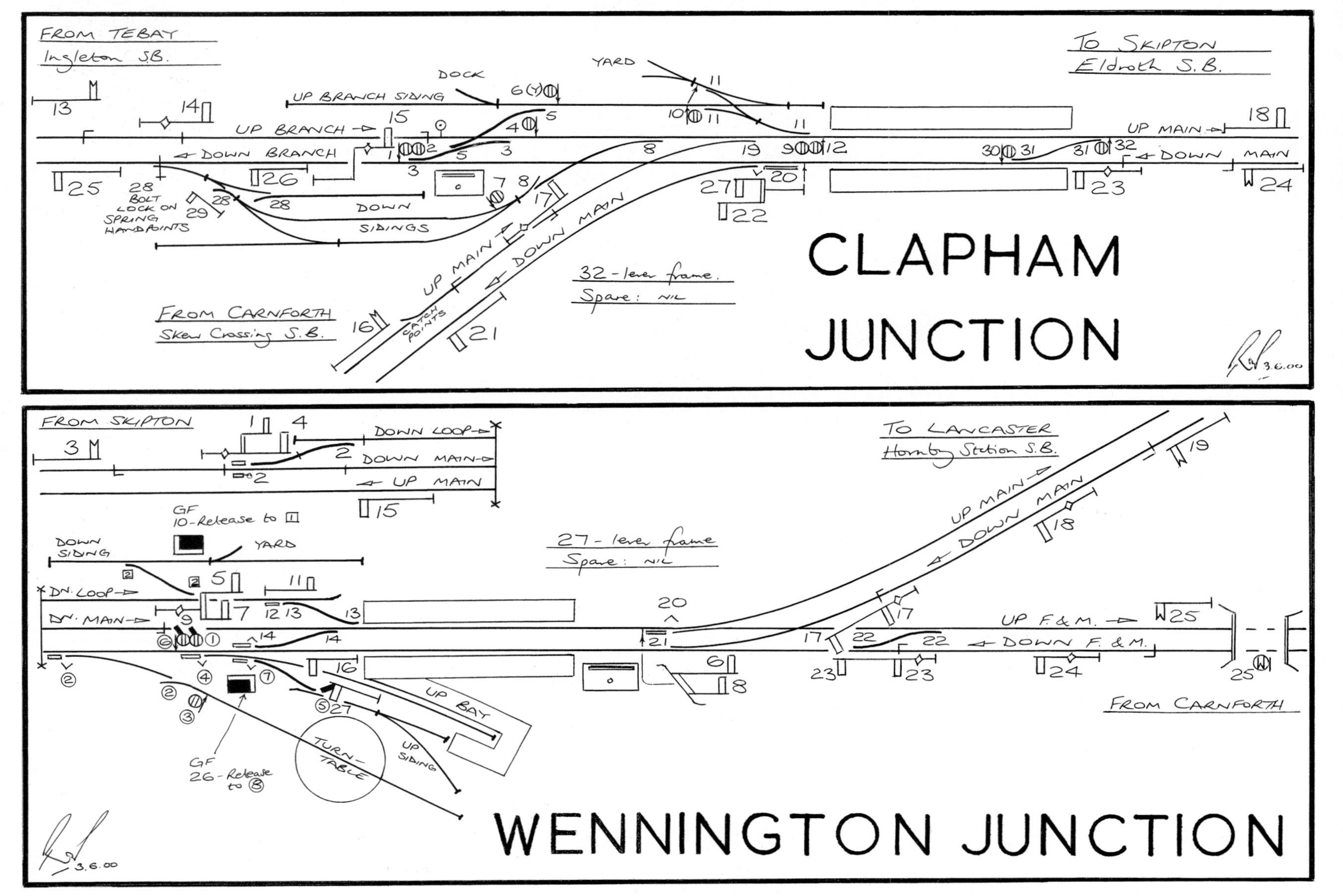

FROM TEBAY
Ingleton S.B.
TO SKIPTON
Eldroth S.B.
DOCK
YARD
UP BRANCH SIDING
UP BRANCH
DOWN BRANCH
UP MAIN
DOWN MAIN
28 BOLT LOCK ON SPRING HANDPOINTS
DOWN SIDINGS
CATCH POINTS
32-lever frame.
Spare: NIL
FROM CARNFORTH
Skew Crossing S.B.
CLAPHAM JUNCTION
3.6.00
FROM SKIPTON
DOWN LOOP
DOWN MAIN
UP MAIN
TO LANCASTER
Hornby Station S.B.
GF 10-Release to 11
DOWN SIDING
YARD
27-lever frame
Spare: NIL
DN. LOOP
DN. MAIN
UP F.&M.
DOWN F.&M.
UP BAY
UP SIDING
TURN-TABLE
GF 26-Release to 8
FROM CARNFORTH
WENNINGTON JUNCTION
3.6.00

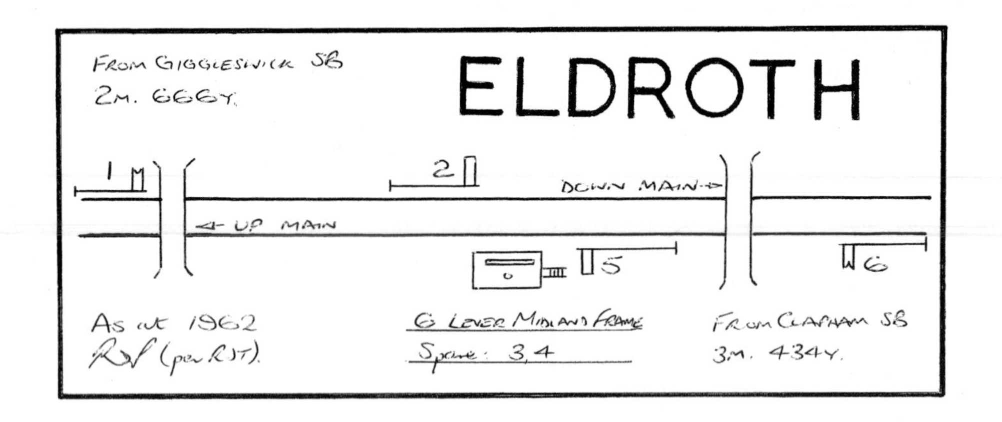

Eldroth box split the block section between Giggleswick and Clapham. It was manned 24 hours per day. There was a fair amount of freight passing during the night. Bell Codes 4 and 3-1 are the passenger trains. The train register extract is for Friday 5 October 1956. *(R.J. Talbot)*

UP LINE Bell Code	UP LINE Train Passed	DOWN LINE Bell Code	DOWN LINE Train Passed
	G. Metcalf on duty 10pm (Thursday)		
	Giggleswick box closed 10pm		
	Distant signals and lights correct 10pm		
1-4	10.35 pm	4	10.41 pm
1-4	10.48	4-1	1.16 am
1-2-2	11.41	1-4	2.09
2-3	12.20 am	4-1	2.25
1-4	3.15	3-1	2.53
1-4	3.35	4-1	3.22
1-4	4.05	4-1	5.33
1-4	5.20		
	G. Metcalf off duty 6am		
	A. D. Oversby on duty 6am		
	Distant signals and lights correct 6am		
4	7.09	2-3	6.16
4-1	7.37	4-1	6.59
		4-1	7.38
	Giggleswick box open 7.30am		
3-1	7.50	3-1	7.57
4	8.26	1-4	8.28
3-1	9.02	4-1	8.46
	Clock correct 9am		
1-4	9.46	4-1	9.01
2-3	10.02	1-4	9.25
3-1	10.38	4-1	9.52
4	11.16	3-1	10.13
3-2	11.28	1-2-2	10.52
1-4	12.09 pm	3-1	12.09 pm
1-4	12.44		
3-1	1.31		
1-4	1.53		
	A. D. Oversby off duty 2pm		
	E. Halliday on duty 2pm		
	Distant signals and light correct 2pm		
2-3	2.07	4-1	2.38
1-4	2.43	1-4	2.55
3	2.57	4	3.15
4	3.35	1-2-2	4.07
5	3.55	1-3-1	4.23
3-1	5.24	3-1	4.51
3-1	5.51	1-4	5.06
1-4	6.13	1-4	5.43
1-4	7.04	4	6.13
3-1	8.00	4	6.18
2-3	9.26	3-1	6.35
1-2-2	10.04	2-3	6.43
		4-1	6.59
		3-1	7.30
		4-1	8.08
		4-1	8.26
		1-4	8.51
	E. Halliday off duty 10pm		
	G. Metcalf on duty 10pm		
	Giggleswick box closed 10pm		
	Distant signals and lights correct 10pm		
3-2	10.22	4	10.44
1-4	10.42		
1-4	11.11		
1-4	11.30		
1-2-2	11.48		

Morecambe Promenade

The first Morecambe station was a temporary affair near to the jetty. In 1851, a permanent structure was opened in Northumberland Street, about 1/2 mile short of the end of the line.

Northumberland Street was too small for the developing traffic and was replaced on 24 March 1907 by Promenade Station. This had two long island platforms, one covered the other open. There was a large concourse at right angles to the platforms with offices facing the sea front.

Associated works included the provision of two independent tracks from the station to the Heysham branch. The goods yard was on the north side of the station and there were carriage sidings. On the south side of the station, the Railway built its own laundry to service the Midland Hotel and the Heysham steamers.

Promenade was convenient for the sea front but was a little way from the town centre. In the mid 1960s, it was suggested that the station might be closed in favour of the London & North Western terminus at Euston Road (see later chapter).

Nothing happened until 1994 when Promenade closed on 6 February. There was then no rail service into Morecambe until 29 May when the present island platform opened close to where the pre 1907 Northumberland Street had been.

The main building at Promenade has been converted into a restaurant and tourist information office.

A 'Black Five' shunting at Morecambe Promenade in July 1964. A train of container flats in the siding. *(Peter Sunderland)*

Morecambe Promenade on 11 September 1991. Only two platforms are in use. Even they are beginning to look overgrown. Class 108 unit 51917 + 54272 is going to Lancaster. *(F.W. Smith)*

The Station concourse on 11 September 1991. No queues for the toilets. The ladies, behind the kiosk is boarded up. *(F.W. Smith)*

Morecambe Promenade exterior in 1991. Today it is fully restored and in use as a restaurant. *(F.W. Smith)*

45675 'Hardy' leads a Morecambe Promenade to Crewe working in July 1964. It is passing Euston Road Station, then in use only as carriage sidings.
(Peter Sunderland)

A somewhat rusty 44912 prepares to leave Morecambe Promenade for Leeds on 27 March 1967. The wires are down but the gantries still up.
(Martin Bairstow Collection)

The new station building at Morecambe. When it is closed, including summer Sundays, there is nowhere at all to shelter on the station.
(F.W. Smith)

Morecambe signal box, 1991. It closed three years later.
(F.W. Smith)

No. 3 ground frame still in place if not in use, 1991. The points were too far away to be pulled from the signal box.
(F.W. Smith)

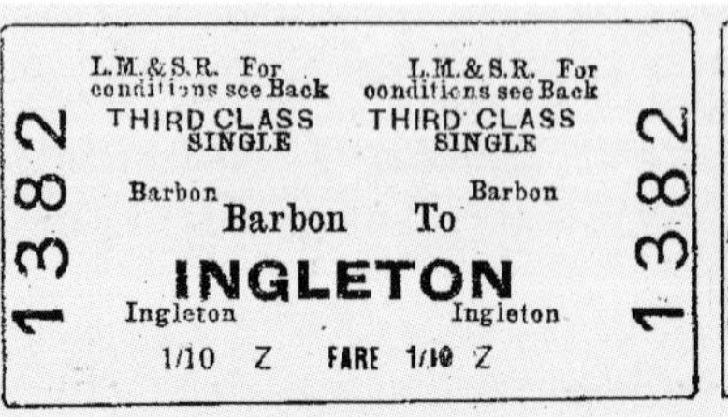

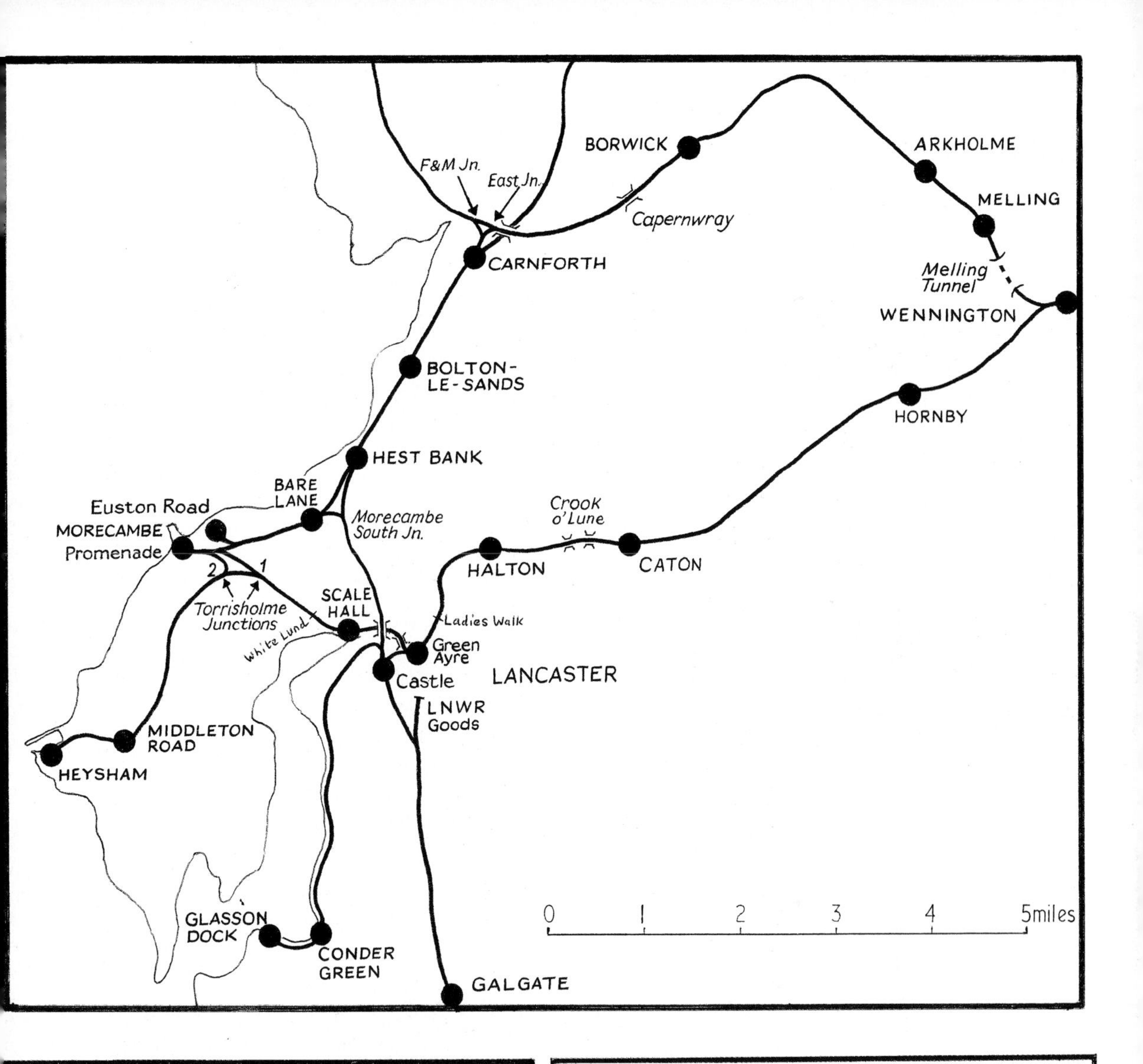

HALF-DAY EXCURSIONS

— TO —

MORECAMBE

FROM	Sundays, July 5, 12, 19 & 26.	Wednesdays, July 1, 8, and 15.	Wednesdays, July 22 and 29.
LEEDS (Wellington) ...... dep.	**10 30 a.m.**	**11 0 a.m.**	**11 25 a.m.**
Morecambe (Prom.) ... arr.	12 55 p.m.	1 29 p.m.	1 38 p.m.
Returning same day from— **Morecambe (Prom.)**..... at	**8 55** p.m.	**8 40** p.m.	**8 40** p.m.
Due to arrive— LEEDS (Wellington) ... ,,	11 15 p.m.	11 2 p.m.	10 56 p.m.

These trains will call at Armley each date on the return journey.

RETURN FARE THIRD CLASS.

4/6

HALF-DAY EXCURSIONS

TO

Clapham, Ingleton, Kirkby Lonsdale, Sedbergh Penrith, Patterdale and Keswick

(ULLSWATER)

FROM	Times of Departure. Sunday, July 19.	Times of Departure. Wednesdays, July 15 and 29. **Dining Car Excursions.**	3rd Class Return Fares. Rail Fare only.	3rd Class Return Fares. * Rail Fare Luncheon outward Supper return.
			s. d.	s. d.
LEEDS (Wellington) .... dep.	**10 0 a.m.**	**11 25 a.m.**	—	—
Clapham .... arr.	11 18 ,,	12 58 p.m.	**3 6**	—
Ingleton .... ,,	11 28 ,,	1 10 ,,	**4 0**	—
Kirkby Lonsdale .... ,,	11 40 ,,	—	**4 0**	—
Sedbergh .... ,,	12 0 noon	1 37 ,,	**4 6**	**9 6**
Penrith .... ,,	12 53 p.m.	2 25 ,,	**5 6**	**10 6**
Patterdale .... ,,	2 40 ,,	3†40 ,,	**8 0**	**13 0**
Keswick .... ,,	1 35 ,,	3 11 ,,	**6 6**	**11 6**

Passengers return same day as shown below :—

From	Sunday, July 19.	Wednesdays, July 15 and 29. Dining Car Excursions.
	p.m.	p.m.
Keswick .... dep.	**6 5**	**7 30**
Patterdale .... ,,	**5 0**	**6†30**
Penrith .... ,,	**7 0**	**8 30**
Sedbergh .... ,,	**7 55**	**9 18**
Kirkby Lonsdale .... ,,	**8 15**	—
Ingleton .... ,,	**8 25**	**9 40**
Clapham .... ,,	**8 38**	**9 53**
LEEDS (Wellington) .... arr.	10 3	11 25

*—Tickets for the **inclusive** booking to cover both Rail Journey and Meals are limited in number, and it is essential that these tickets be obtained in advance, as no increase can be made in the number of Inclusive Rail and Meal Tickets. †—Arrives 4.15 p.m. and returns 7.0 p.m. on July 29th.

Summer Timetable

The table which follows is taken from the July 1938 *Bradshaw.* It shows the Monday to Friday passenger service based on departures from Skipton. The Saturday service was more intense, Sunday less so. Skipton departures for the Settle & Carlisle line are excluded.

Summer 1938 – Mondays to Fridays Departures from Skipton for the 'Little' North Western Line

	am	
	7.07	All stations to Morecambe Promenade and Carnforth
	8.30	Hellifield, Heysham (for Douglas)
	9.30	All stations to Morecambe Promenade and Carnforth
	11.03	All stations to Morecambe Promenade
	11.40	Hellifield, Wennington, then all stations to Carnforth, through carriages to Barrow in Furness
MFO	11.57	Hellifield, Lancaster GA, Morecambe Promenade
	pm	
FO	1.31	Hellifield, Clapham, Carnforth, through carriages to Windermere. Ingleton, Kirkby Lonsdale, Sedbergh through carriages to Keswick
	2.58	Wennington, Melling, Arkholme, Carnforth, through carriages to Barrow in Furness
	3.16	Hellifield, Lancaster GA, Morecambe Promenade
	3.23	All stations to Morecambe Promenade
	4.07	All stations to Morecambe Promenade
	4.38	Hellifield, Clapham, Wennington, Arkholme, Borwick, Carnforth
	5.25	All stations to Wennington, Lancaster GA, Morecambe Promenade, Arkholme, Borwick, Carnforth
	5.38	Lancaster GA, Morecambe Promenade
	5.47	All stations to Wennington, Lancaster GA, Morecambe Promenade, Arkholme, Carnforth
	6.47	All stations to Morecambe Promenade and, except Borwick, to Carnforth
	9.04	All stations to Bentham, Lancaster GA, Morecambe Promenade
	10.10	Hellifield, Lancaster GA, Heysham (for Belfast)

Most trains were through from Leeds City or Bradford Forster Square.

MFO = Mondays and Fridays only
FO = Fridays only

It was on a summer Saturday, that the service became really intense with additional trains taking holidaymakers to Morecambe and beyond.

Instead of amalgamating at Shipley, the Leeds and Bradford portions of the 'Isle of Man Boat Express' ran as separate trains. The 7.35am from Leeds City called only at Bingley, Keighley and Hellifield to arrive at Heysham at 9.31. The 7.48 from Bradford Forster Square called at Shipley, Bingley, Keighley, Skipton and Hellifield to arrive ten minutes behind the Leeds train. Following a few minutes later was the 7.40am from Leeds City calling at Armley, Kirkstall, Newlay, Calverley & Rodley, Apperley Bridge then not stop to Skipton and Morecambe Promenade (arrive 9.46am). Close behind was the 8.06 from Bradford Forster Square, all stations to Keighley then Morecambe Promenade (arrive 9.53am). Next was the 8.20 from Bradford serving Manningham, Shipley, Bingley, Keighley, Hellifield, Skipton and Morecambe Promenade (arrive 10.10am). Then the 7.50 from Leeds City calling at Armley, Kirkstall, Newlay, Calverley & Rodley, Skipton and Morecambe Promenade (10.16).

There was a 9.15 from Leeds, calling at Apperley Bridge, Bingley, Keighley, Skipton, Lancaster Green Ayre, arriving Morecambe Promenade at 11.15. This was followed by a through train from Heeley, just south of Sheffield which avoided Leeds but then stopped at Keighley, Skipton, Lancaster and Morecambe (arrive 11.25). Next at 9.30 from Leeds was the 'Belfast Boat Express' calling at Keighley, Skipton then non stop to Heysham for the daylight sailing which reached Belfast Donegall Quay at 7.30pm.

At 9.34 from Leeds and 9.38 from Bradford, there was a through train to Barrow in Furness. The two portions joined at Shipley, called at Bingley, Keighley and Skipton then ran non stop to Carnforth East Junction where the front coaches were detached for Carnforth itself whilst the rear portion went on to Barrow.

At 10.25 from Leeds, there was a through express from Nottingham. This served Skipton, Hellifield, Lancaster and Morecambe (arrive 12.25).

There was a 10.41 from Bradford to Carnforth which ran as an independent train on Saturdays. On Mondays to Fridays carriages from Bradford joined the Leeds to Barrow train at Shipley (11.40 from Skipton). There was a further Saturdays only Bradford to Morecambe train at 11.02. Then at 11.50 from Leeds and 12.02 from Bradford, there was another 'Isle of Man Boat Express', joining at Shipley and calling at Bingley, Keighley, Skipton, then non stop to Heysham for the sailing which reached Douglas at 7pm.

There was the 'Bradford & Morecambe Residential Express' at 12.45, a year round Saturday working. Then the through train from Sheffield and Leeds to Windermere and Keswick, the same as the Friday train (1.31 from Skipton). Then a 1.24pm non stop from Leeds City to Morecambe Promenade arrive 3.11 closely followed by the 1.37 from Bradford Forster Square to Morecambe which stopped only at Keighley. There was another Saturdays only Bradford to Morecambe at 2.25 calling most stations to Skipton then non stop to Morecambe arrive 4.15. Behind this was a 2.10 from Manchester Victoria calling various stations to Blackburn then non stop via Hellifield to Lancaster Green Ayre and Morecambe Promenade.

After this, the Saturday timetable settled down to something like a normal weekday.

The 'Residential'

The 5.38pm from Skipton was the return working of the 'Leeds, Bradford & Morecambe Residential'. At that time there was a flow of long distance commuters from Morecambe to the West Riding, Bradford in particular. The people concerned were of the executive or proprietorial class who didn't need to be in their offices until 9.30 or later.

The 'Resi' left Morecambe Prom at 7.42am Mondays to Saturdays calling at Lancaster Green Ayre and Skipton where it split for Bradford Forster Square (arrive 9.15) and Leeds City (arrive 9.26). The Leeds portion stopped at Keighley. Mondays to Fridays the return was at 4.55pm from Leeds and 5.10 from Bradford. On Saturdays, the return was from Bradford only at 12.45. The working was long standing. Times in 1910 had been very similar. In 1964 they were still almost identical.

Then came the rerouting in January 1966 which knocked out the Lancaster stop. The through Bradford portion was another casualty. The 1976 timetable shows a dmu leaving Morecambe at 7.40am all stations to Leeds arrive 9.48. Bradford passengers had to change at Keighley to reach Forster Square at 9.38am. The return working is at 17.12 from Leeds arriving Morecambe at 19.23. Bradford customers could leave at 17.15 changing at Keighley.

Today, if there were any Bradford wool magnates living in Morecambe, they would have to leave at 6.27am, change at Lancaster and Shipley to reach Bradford at 9.09.

Patriot 4-6-0 No. 45518 'Bradshaw' pauses at Lancaster Green Ayre with a Morecambe to Leeds semi fast on 17 March 1962. *(P. B. Booth/N. E. Stead Collection)*

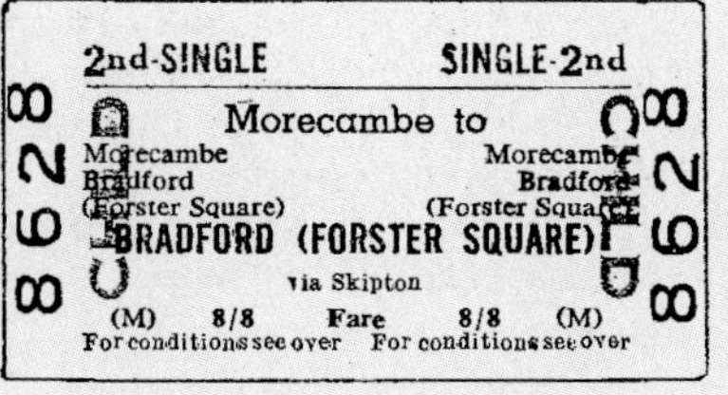

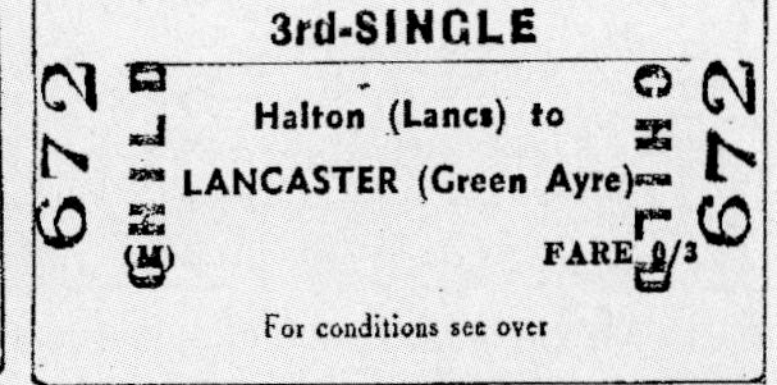

AMENDED ISSUE. P 21 M.

L M S

LONDON MIDLAND AND SCOTTISH RAILWAY.

SUMMER RESIDENTIAL EXPRESSES.

WEEK-DAYS,

July 20th to September 13th, 1931,

MORECAMBE, BRADFORD and LEEDS.

MORNING SERVICE.

		a.m.
MORECAMBE (Promenade)	dep.	7 42
SHIPLEY - - - - -	arr.	- -
BRADFORD (Forster Square)	,,	9 15
LEEDS (Wellington) - -	,,	9 28

EVENING RETURN SERVICE.

		S p.m.
LEEDS (Wellington) - -	dep.	4 55
BRADFORD (Forster Square)	,,	5 10
SHIPLEY - - - - -	,,	5 16
MORECAMBE (Promenade)	arr.	6 40

S—**Saturdays excepted.** For full Service of Trains see Time Tables.

July, 1931. **J. H. FOLLOWS, Vice-President.**

(100—5,000) McCorquodale & Co., Ltd., Printers, London and Newton.—1997

M 2638

L M S

LONDON MIDLAND AND SCOTTISH RAILWAY.

Saturdays, June 28 and July 5, 1930,

PERIOD EXCURSION TICKETS

TO

DOUGLAS (Isle of Man)

Via Heysham and the Isle of Man S.P. Coy.'s Steamers.

FROM	Times of Departure.	RETURN FARES. Third and Saloon.	Third Class Throughout.
	a.m.	s. d.	s. d.
Kendal	7 43	24 0	16 6
Oxenholme	8 15	23 9	16 3
Barrow	7 5	26 3	18 9
Dalton	7 15	25 6	18 0
Ulverston	7 27	24 9	17 3
Grange	7 41	23 0	15 6
Arnside	7 48	22 6	15 0
Carnforth	8 40	21 6	14 0
Lancaster (Castle)	8 53	20 6	13 0
Lancaster (Green Ayre)	9 0	20 3	12 9
Heysham (Boat)	10 0	—	—
DOUGLAS arr. about	1 0 p.m.	—	—

RETURN ARRANGEMENTS.

Passengers return on any weekday up to and including 15 days from date of outward journey from Douglas (Victoria Pier) at 4.0 p.m. going forward from Heysham at 8.0 p.m., connecting with the 8.38 p.m. train from Lancaster (Green Ayre).

Passengers booking outward on July 5th, may also return from Douglas (Victoria Pier) at 9.0 a.m. on July 19th.

Children under 3 years of age free; 3 and under 14 half-fares.

LUGGAGE ALLOWANCE.

Passengers holding Period Excursion Tickets are allowed free conveyance of personal Luggage not exceeding 100 lbs. in weight, and in order to prevent loss of or delay, it is requested that all old labels be removed or defaced, and that the packages be fully and legibly addressed. For further security the owner's full name and address should be placed in each package.

Conditions of Issue of Excursion and other Reduced Fare Tickets.
Excursion Tickets, and Tickets issued at Fares less than the Ordinary Fares, are issued subject to the Notices and Conditions shewn in the Company's current Time Tables.

Tickets, Bills and all particulars may be obtained in advance at the Stations, or from the following:—

BARROW—Messrs. Thos. Cook & Son, Ltd., 61, Duke Street.

Or on application to the Divisional Passenger Commercial Superintendent, Hunt's Bank, Manchester.

J. H. FOLLOWS, Vice-President.

May, 1930. (Com. XM 48561/A)

(5,000) McCorquodale & Co., Ltd., Printers, London and Newton.—1722 **M 2638**

'Black Five' No. 45273 negotiates Wennington Junction with a Morecambe to Leeds semi fast about 1962.
(N. E. Stead Collection)

Excursion traffic

In August 1950, Sir Eustace Missenden, Chairman of British Railways, addressed a press conference called to unveil the forthcoming Winter timetable. Much of what he had to say was concerned with progress in the return to normality after the war. Besides promising such comforts as soap and water in sleeping cars, he pledged 'the continuation of excursion trips for those of modest means'. Noting that 10 million passengers a year patronised excursion trains, he confirmed that 1,500 specials would be taking visitors to the Autumn illuminations at Morecambe, Blackpool and Southend.

Throughout that Summer, the Bradford *Telegraph & Argus* carried an advertisement every Thursday listing forthcoming excursions. It only gave the departure time and fare, usually in the case of Morecambe trips, from Bradford Forster Square and Apperley Bridge. Corresponding ads appeared in papers such as the *Keighley News*. Day excursions cost 7s 6d, half day only 6s 3d. Different series of Edmondson card tickets were needed for each, probably with the appropriate child issues as well. Failing that they would have to cut a ticket diagonally in half for a child. There were no reductions for senior citizens at that time.

Half day trips to Morecambe became especially popular after 15 August when George Formby switched on the illuminations. On Saturday 9 September, for example, there was a trip leaving Bradford Forster Square at 1.15pm which cost the full 7s 6d. If you only wanted to pay 6s 3d, you had to wait until the 4.10pm departure. Outside the illuminations season, 1.15pm might have qualified for a half day fare but the stay in Morecambe was prolonged into the late evening allowing patrons to enjoy 'the lights'.

This created a problem for people who didn't live within walking distance of their originating station if they arrived back too late for connecting trains or buses. Special late buses were provided at Bradford Forster Square. To assess demand, Bradford City Transport staff were on hand before the excursion departed and passengers were asked to make their requirements known at that stage.

Occasionally, trains picked up at stations normally closed to passengers. On Sunday 3 September there was a trip to Morecambe from Idle and Eccleshill, both closed in 1931, which then picked up at Queensbury and Thornton before joining the Midland route at Keighley. On Saturday 19 August, the residents of Yeadon were offered a trip to Morecambe. The station there had never seen a regular passenger service. As more stations closed during the 1950s, the practice continued of stopping excursions at places with no regular service.

An Ivatt 2-6-0 crossing Waterside Viaduct, north of Sedbergh, with a ramblers' excursion from Bradford Forster Square to Tebay in April 1960. *(Peter Sunderland)*

4F No. 44562 accelerates away from Keighley with a Morecambe excursion in 1954. The arc roof non corridor coaches are of Midland origin. The 4F is less likely to stall on the return journey than might a 3F.
(Peter Sunderland)

By September 1963, excursionists had every hope of surmounting the gradients plus the luxury of access to the loo. A class 104 negotiates Clapham Junction on a Leeds to Morecambe illuminations special.
(Peter Sunderland)

'Jubilee' class No. 45646 'Napier' taking the Lancaster line at Clapham with a Leeds-Morecambe express in September 1963.
(Peter Sunderland)

A 'Black Five' crossing Low Gill Viaduct in April 1960 with a return Tebay to Leeds excursion made up of non corridor coaches.
(Peter Sunderland)

Morecambe was not the only destination reached by excursions over the 'Little' North Western route. On Sunday 18 June 1950, both Bradford Forster Square and Apperley Bridge offered bookings to Arnside, Grange-Over-Sands, Lakeside, Bowness and Ambleside. The last two destinations were by Windermere lake steamer from Lakeside. The Bradford and Leeds portions would have joined at either Keighley or Skipton.

Within half an hour, this excursion was followed by one for ramblers visiting Clapham, Ingleton, Kirkby Lonsdale, Barbon and Sedbergh, again with portions from both Leeds City and Bradford Forster Square. Another destination appearing from time to time during the Summer was Barrow in Furness with stops at Arnside, Grange and Ulverston.

A variation on the theme was a trip on Sunday 9 July to both Lakeside (Windermere) and Morecambe with time in each. This started from Bradford Exchange picking up at various stations en route to Keighley via Queensbury.

The first two weeks in August were Bowling Tide when the mills and factories closed down in Bradford allowing many people to take their annual holiday. On Fridays 4 and 11 August there was an extra train to Morecambe at 5.10pm from Forster Square. Then, the following morning there were extras at 7.00, 7.25, 8.00, 8.13, 9.25 and 9.55am.

During Bowling Tide, day excursions from Bradford moved onto mid week days. A similar exodus happened from other towns during their various wakes weeks but Morecambe received its biggest influx from Bradford.

Peter Sunderland was an occasional excursionist to Morecambe. His first problem, living at Haworth, was that trips were no good if they got back to Keighley too late for the last transport up the Worth Valley. On a handful of days each year, the train ran through from Oxenhope. The return journey could still be a frustrating experience, even an agonising one in non-corridor coaches. If the coal was of poor quality, the loco might run short of steam on the climb up to Clapham. The train wouldn't normally stop in a station. It would just stall at the point where the loco could no longer create enough vacuum to hold the brakes off. If it did happen to be in a station, some passengers would rush to the toilet but you didn't know how long the train would be stood there and were frightened of missing it.

A loco which had stalled on the modest gradient towards Clapham was quite likely to run out of steam again on the 1 in 56 between Ingrow and Oakworth. So close to home but another stand waiting for the pressure to build up again. In early post war years, the engine would be a Midland 3F hauling old LMS compartment coaches or even arc roof Midland stock. By the 1950s, 4Fs were more usual. In 1956 a 'crab' appeared on an Oxenhope to Morecambe excursion. The coaches were stored in wayside sidings and sometimes the batteries were flat so, if the train stopped, the light would go out.

People would put up with this after six years of war but for how long? Some deserted the railway in favour of buses and coaches. But it was the growth of car ownership which ended the mass movement of passengers by rail to resorts such as Morecambe.

Excursions provided variety for observers of the railway scene. During 1956, ex LNER engines were noted on Morecambe excursions. In June, B1 No. 61240 worked a schools special but next day a Starbeck based 'Hunt', No. 62738 'The Zetland' turned up in Morecambe. On 8 July, B1 No.61306 worked a ramblers excursion from Hull to Ingleton from where the loco returned to Hellifield Shed for servicing. Bank Holiday Monday saw 'Jubilee' No 45698 'Mars' on a ramblers excursion to Kirkby Lonsdale. An unusual working on 16 August 1958 was 8F 2-8-0 No 48311 of Stourton Shed on a return Morecambe to Holmfirth excursion, routed via Ilkley.

The Beeching Report called for the scrapping of rolling stock maintained only for excursion and holiday traffic. By the late 1960s it had mostly gone.

There was a new type of excursion in the 1970s – the 'Merrymaker' which took people long distances in reasonable comfort at fares lower in real terms than those of the traditional seaside excursion. As an example, on 12 August 1975, I travelled from Bradford Forster Square to Pitlochry and back (684 miles) on a day excursion. Whilst we were travelling that distance, Morecambe was receiving its own long distance 'Merrymakers'. Then BR clamped down on this activity and it died by about 1980.

Of course, one can still take a day trip to Morecambe, as we did in the opening chapter. But we were hardly part of a mass movement. This is confirmed by the small size of the new Morecambe station. The toilets alone in the old Promenade Station were bigger than the entire new building. They had to be with all those people arriving in compartment coaches.

D 2667

LMS

LONDON MIDLAND AND SCOTTISH RAILWAY

MORECAMBE CARNIVAL

SATURDAYS, SEPT. 12th to SEPT. 19th, 1931

CHEAP RETURN TICKETS

FIRST AND THIRD CLASS

At about the SINGLE FARE (plus fractional parts of 1d.)

WILL BE ISSUED

EACH DAY

TO

MORECAMBE

From any L M S STATION within a RADIUS of 60 Miles

The Tickets will be available on the OUTWARD and RETURN JOURNEYS by any Ordinary Train the same day.

CONDITIONS OF ISSUE OF EXCURSION TICKETS AND OTHER REDUCED FARE TICKETS.
Excursion tickets and tickets issued at fares less than the ordinary fares are issued subject to the Notices and Conditions shewn in the Company's Current Time Tables.

All information regarding Excursion Trains on the London Midland and Scottish Railway can be obtained on application to the Divisional Passenger Commercial Superintendent, Hunt's Bank, Manchester, and General Superintendent (Passenger Commercial), Derby.

PLEASE RETAIN THIS BILL FOR REFERENCE.

September, 1931. J. H. FOLLOWS, Vice-President.

40,000 H. Bemrose & Sons Ltd., Derby and London.

JULY, 1931, ISSUE. D 2194

L M S

LONDON MIDLAND AND SCOTTISH RAILWAY.

WEDNESDAYS and SATURDAYS

Commencing JULY 22nd, 1931, until further notice.

COOK'S CHEAP TICKETS to

GARGRAVE, BELL BUSK, GIGGLESWICK SETTLE, CLAPHAM, BENTHAM INGLETON & WENNINGTON

FROM	Times of Departure.			FROM	Times of Departure.		
	a.m.	a.m.	Sats. only. p.m.		a.m.	a.m.	Sats. only. p.m.
LEEDS (Wellington)	6 10	9 23	12A12	BRADFORD (Forster Sq.)	6 5	9 48	12A45
KIRKSTALL	—	9 30	12A24	MANNINGHAM	6 9	9 52	12A41
NEWLAY	—	9 35	12A29	FRIZINGHALL	6 12	9 55	12A44
CALVERLEY	—	9 39	12A33	SHIPLEY	6 15	10 1	12A52
APPERLEY BRIDGE	6 23	9 44	12A38	GUISELEY	—	9 45	12A 9

A—No bookings to Giggleswick, Bentham and Wennington by this train. Gargrave, Bell Busk and Settle passengers leave Skipton at 1.28 p.m.

RETURN FARES TO—

FROM	Gargrave.		Bell Busk.		Giggleswick or Settle.		Clapham.		Bentham or Ingleton.		Wennington.	
	1st.	3rd.	1st.	3rd.	1st.	3rd.	1st.	3rd.	1st.	3rd.	1st.	3rd.
	s. d.	s. d.	s. d.	s. d.	s. d.	s. d.	s. d.	s. d.	s. d.	s. d.	s. d.	s. d.
LEEDS	6 3	3 9	6 11	4 2	8 7	5 2	9 10	5 11	10 8	6 5	11 5	6 10
KIRKSTALL	5 8	3 5	6 3	3 9	8 1	4 10	9 2	5 8	10 0	6 0	10 9	6 6
NEWLAY	5 4	3 3	6 0	3 7	7 9	4 8	8 11	5 4	9 10	5 11	10 5	6 3
CALVERLEY	5 2	3 1	5 8	3 5	7 6	4 6	8 9	5 3	9 6	5 9	10 3	6 2
APPERLEY	4 9	2 10	5 4	3 3	7 1	4 3	8 3	5 0	9 2	5 6	10 0	6 0
BRADFORD	4 7	2 9	5 3	3 2	7 0	4 3	8 2	4 11	9 1	5 6	9 9	5 10
MANNINGHAM	4 5	2 8	5 0	3 0	6 10	4 1	7 11	4 9	8 11	5 4	9 6	5 9
FRIZINGHALL	4 4	2 7	4 10	2 11	6 7	4 0	7 10	4 9	8 8	5 3	9 4	5 7
SHIPLEY	4 1	2 6	4 7	2 9	6 5	3 10	7 8	4 7	8 6	5 1	9 2	5 6
GUISELEY	4 6	2 9	5 2	3 1	6 11	4 2	8 1	4 10	8 11	5 4	9 8	5 10

CHILDREN under three years of age, free; three years and under fourteen, half-fares.

PASSENGERS RETURN SAME DAY BY ANY TRAIN AFTER 4.0 p.m.

Passengers are requested to OBTAIN their TICKETS IN ADVANCE, as this will assist the Company in the provision of accommodation.

Tickets can be purchased at the Stations; also at the following Offices:—

BRADFORD.—Thos. Cook & Son, Ltd., 21, Market Street; A. Altham, Ltd., 21, Westgate, and 140, Manchester Road; Bradford Co-operative Society, 65, Sunbridge Road.

LEEDS.—Messrs. Thos. Cook & Son, Ltd., 55, Boar Lane; Messrs. A. Altham, Ltd., 4, New Market Street, 255, Hunslet Road, and 34a, Tong Road; Travellers, Ltd., 5, Boar Lane.

SHIPLEY.—The WINDHILL CO-OPERATIVE SOCIETY, Market Place.

CONDITIONS OF ISSUE OF EXCURSION TICKETS AND OTHER REDUCED FARE TICKETS.
Excursion tickets and tickets issued at fares less than the ordinary fares are issued subject to the Notices and Conditions shewn in the Company's Current Time Tables.

CHEAP DAY TICKETS BY ORDINARY TRAINS.—Passengers may take with them, free of charge at Owner's Risk, goods for their own personal use not exceeding 120 lbs. (1st Class) or 60 lbs. (3rd Class).

All information regarding Excursion Trains on the London Midland and Scottish Railway can be obtained on application to the Divisional Passenger Commercial Superintendent, Hunt's Bank, Manchester, and General Superintendent (Passenger Commercial), Derby.

PLEASE RETAIN THIS BILL FOR REFERENCE.

July, 1931. (C.X.D. 2/3414) J. H. FOLLOWS, Vice-President.

8,000 H., 60 P. Bemrose & Sons Ltd., Derby and London.

The London & North Western Railway at Morecambe

Morecambe Euston Road about 1920. *(Sankey Collection)*

In 1859 the Lancaster & Carlisle Railway deposited a Bill for a three mile line roughly following the William Lands branch abandoned a decade earlier. It was to leave the L&C main line at Hest Bank and run to a junction with the 'Little' North Western just outside Morecambe station. There was to be a branch from Bare Lane leading out onto a jetty about a mile to the east of the existing harbour. The Bill also sought running powers over the harbour lines and port facilities belonging to the 'Little' North Western Railway.

The junction at Hest Bank faced northward confirming that the scheme was not primarily for a passenger line which would surely have run direct from Lancaster. The main aim was to carry coke and iron ore between County Durham and the sea. This traffic came onto the Lancaster & Carlisle Railway at Tebay. With the help of the proposed new line, it would be able to reach the sea at Morecambe without recourse to travelling over the 'Little' North Western.

The latter company retaliated with its own Bill proposing the alternative of a north to west curve half a mile in length from the Lancaster & Carlisle to its own line near Scale Hall.

A costly Parliamentary battle was avoided when the two sides compromised. The Lancaster & Carlisle withdrew its harbour branch and demands for running powers. The 'Little' North Western dropped its own Bill and didn't oppose the watered down Lancaster & Carlisle measure which was duly passed in August 1859.

After all that there was no early start on building the modest line. By the time it opened on 13 August 1864, the Lancaster & Carlisle had become part of the London & North Western Railway.

Agreement could not be reached on the use of the 'Little' North Western station at Morecambe. Instead, LNWR trains terminated at a station called Poulton Lane on its own territory.

In 1886 the LNWR opened a more substantial terminus at Euston Road. It was situated on a short branch part way between Poulton Lane and the junction with the Midland. The station was built with yellow bricks. It had one covered platform nearest the main building and four platforms open to the elements. These were needed for the growing number of holiday and excursion trains which also required siding accommodation. This was provided at Balloon Sidings near to the redundant Poulton Lane Station. The curve from Morecambe South Junction to Bare Lane opened on 19 May 1888.

The regular year round service from Morecambe Euston Road was to Lancaster Castle calling at Bare Lane. In 1910 there were 17 departures from Morecambe each weekday between 5.30am and

9.40pm. There were only two on a Sunday, both in the early evening.

This standard of service continued until the mid 1950s. When the electric trains were reintroduced on the Midland route in March 1956, the ex LNWR steam service was reduced virtually to peak hours only.

Euston Road closed in September 1958 and local trains were diverted to Promenade Station. They returned to Euston Road during the 1959 summer timetable but used Promenade permanently from September 1959. During the summers of 1960, 1961 and 1962, Euston Road was opened only for excursions and long distance Saturday trains. After that, the station was not used again.

The winter 1960/61 timetable shows a further reduction in the Lancaster to Morecambe service via Bare Lane creating quite a number of empty stock workings.

From **Lancaster Castle**	From **Morecambe Promenade**
9.50 am	6.30 am
4.23 pm	6.55 am
5.25 pm	7.32 am
6.00 pm	8.00 am
6.42 pm	8.30 am
	9.55 am
	12.00 noon SO
	2.30 pm
	4.58 pm
SUNDAYS	
11.20 am	10.45 am
9.15 pm	12.00 noon
	7.05 pm

All trains stopped at Bare Lane. The Heysham boat trains are not included.

From 3 January 1966, the service from between Lancaster Castle, Bare Lane and Morecambe was increased in compensation for closure of the electric line.

A class 110 'Calder Valley' set restarts from Bare Lane with a morning Leeds to Morecambe service on 20 July 1984. *(Martin Bairstow)*

Euston Road in use only for stabling carriages in December 1965. (Geoffrey Lewthwaite)

Passenger Sailings from Morecambe

Despite severe tidal restrictions, Morecambe functioned as a cross channel port from 1851 until 1904.
(Martin Bairstow Collection)

Part of the Morecambe Harbour & Railway scheme was the construction of what has always been known as the stone jetty. According to *North of Leeds,* this was built with only a vague similarity to the works authorised by the 1846 Act. It was re-authorised retrospectively by the North Western Railway Act 1852. The jetty was actually close to completion by February 1851.

A paddle steamer called 'Albion' sailed to Piel, near Barrow, in association with the Furness Railway. Until 1857, the Furness Railway relied on steamers from Morecambe and Fleetwood for its link with the rest of the railway network. The steamers declined in importance once the direct railway was opened. They disappeared altogether by 1869.

The Morecambe to Belfast service started in 1851, at first with chartered vessels. The operation was taken over about 1854 by the Midland Railway who bought a ship being built on the Tyne for the Russian Government. Because of the Crimean War, the order was cancelled and the screw driven vessel became 'Arbutus' in the Midland fleet. It worked alongside a paddle steamer called "Laurel".

At first the Belfast sailing was twice weekly with a call at Ramsey, Isle of Man. After the first few years, the Ramsey call was omitted but the frequency increased.

The Midland ships to Belfast were in competition with the joint London & North Western/Lancashire & Yorkshire Railway vessels from Fleetwood. Like Morecambe, Fleetwood was tidal though extensive dredging did allow fixed steamship timetables to operate there from 1894. This goal was never achieved at Morecambe.

The Midland Railway timetable for June 1860 shows an overnight sailing to Belfast five days per week. Departure time varied according to the tide. The journey occupied about 11 hours 'weather permitting'. The service was provided by 'The new and powerful first class iron steam ships 'Laurel', 'Lyra' and 'Arbutus'.

The last named left Morecambe each Wednesday evening direct to Londonderry, returning from there on Friday afternoons. It called off the Giant's Causeway 'weather permitting'. There was no harbour there so passengers would have disembarked by small boat. Cabin fares (first class) were about 2½ times steerage (third class) but were fully inclusive – 'no steward's or other fees'.

A smaller vessel, 'Myrtle' made a return trip on different days to Fleetwood, Grange or Piel (near Barrow).

The Leeds train connecting with the Belfast sailing (sometimes a different train according to the tide) was extended to and from Morecambe Pier where passengers' luggage was transferred free of charge. For those needing to stay overnight in Morecambe, there were 'excellent hotels where passengers will meet with every comfort and attention'. One of these was the Railway's own North Western Hotel, later known as the Midland.

Despite these claims, Morecambe had severe limitations for navigation. With the opening of the Wennington to Carnforth line in 1867, the Midland Railways transferred its Belfast service first to Piel and then in 1881 to Ramsden Dock, Barrow. Here the Furness Railway built a railway station alongside the steamer berth which was outside the Dock itself.

Bradshaw for November 1880 shows the Boat Train leaving London St Pancras at 10.35am. It departs Leeds Wellington at 3.50pm, picks up Bradford coaches at Shipley and makes a leisurely progress. It calls at Bingley, Keighley, Skipton, Hellifield 'New Station', Long Preston 'on Mondays when required to take up for Belfast', Giggleswick, Clapham, Bentham, Wennington, where the Morecambe portion is detached, then Arkholme. It spends 15 minutes at Carnforth before continuing to Grange, Ulverston, Furness Abbey and finally Piel Pier which is reached at 7.20pm.

From Piel 'the swift and powerful first class Royal Mail paddle steam ships 'Tyrone', 'Armagh', 'Roe' and 'Herald' are appointed to sail (weather and unforeseen circumstances permitting) in connection with the through trains of the Midland and Furness Railways.'

The ship is timed to leave at 8pm. The corresponding sailing leaves Belfast at the same time and arrives at Piel (weather etc permitting) in time for the 7.15am 'Boat Train' which reaches Leeds at 10.20am and St Pancras at 3.10pm. In this direction the train is accelerated between Wennington and Leeds with stops only at Skipton, Keighley and Apperley Bridge.

The ships were operated by the Barrow Steam Navigation Company, a joint venture of the Midland and Furness Railways and James Little & Sons, their agents in Belfast.

On 1 October 1881, the ships and connecting trains were diverted from Piel to Ramsden Dock. The route prospered until the Midland Railway opened Heysham Harbour in 1904, somewhat to the disappointment of the Furness Railway. The Barrow to Belfast sailing and connecting trains then continued three days per week until the First World War.

After losing the Railway steamers, Morecambe still retained some sailings right until the opening of Heysham Harbour in 1904. These included the service to Londonderry which Laird Line had revived in the late 1860s following closure of the Midland Railway operation, first begun in 1851. In 1889 Laird Line introduced a twice weekly sailing from Morecambe to Dublin which ran until transfer to Heysham in 1904.

After this the stone jetty was leased by T W Ward of Sheffield who turned the area into a ship breaking yard. This operated for nearly 30 years. Amongst its 'customers' were the White Star liner 'Majestic' and two Isle of Man Steam Packets, 'Ben-My-Chree' and 'Mona's Isle' which made their last single journeys to Morecambe in 1906 and 1919.

The yard occupied a prominent site on the seafront. Wagons loaded with scrap were shunted across the shore road into the goods yard alongside Promenade Station. Until 1926, when the trams closed, the tracks leading onto the jetty made a level crossing with the horse tramway which ran along the seafront between Bare and the Battery Inn.

The scrapyard and railway sidings closed in the early 1930s when Morecambe Corporation purchased the area as part of its Foreshore Improvement Scheme. About the same time, the present Midland Hotel was built on the same site as the previous Midland Hotel. This was the original North Western Hotel of 1851 although it appears to have been extended as Morecambe grew in importance.

During the 1990s the stone jetty was restored and enlarged as part of a new scheme to improve the appearance of Morecambe sea front and to prevent flooding in the town.

Morecambe Harbour was well and truly silted up by 1960. The 'Lunesdale', a Fleetwood to Knott End ferry, has sailed to Morecambe to offer an excursion round the bay. *(Peter Sunderland)*

Heysham Harbour

In 1892, the Midland Railway obtained powers for a branch to Heysham where they intended to build a steamer pier in far deeper water than at Morecambe. Four years later the scheme was enlarged into a major harbour complex, twice the size of that which was eventually opened in 1904. The south quay, upon which the passenger station stands, was intended to be an island between the harbour and a larger inner dock which, in the event, was never built. The nuclear power station is built on what would have been this inner dock.

The harbour is enclosed by two breakwaters which are nearly a mile apart at the shore end but only 300 yards at the harbour mouth. Ships could enter at all states of the tide. The entire complex was powered by electricity.

The branch railway had been opened on 12 November 1898 but only for contractors building the harbour. It was used during the summer of 1904 by holidaymakers viewing the work and the new ships. It opened normally on 1 September 1904 when the entire harbour complex came into use.

In 1896, the Midland Railway bought the Heysham Tower Hotel. Business picked up after the branch railway and harbour opened but in 1914 it was requisitioned for the use of army officers. After the War, the Midland Railway sold it rather than resume normal business there.

In common with many branch lines, Morecambe to Heysham was singled during the First World War but dedoubled afterwards with the compensation received from the Government. It has been single track again since 1994.

The 'Little' North Western port at Morecambe was never satisfactory. In 1904, the Midland Railway opened Heysham Harbour, three miles to the south. One of the three 'Dukes' built in 1928 for the Belfast service is berthed alongside the transit shed. The passenger station is the building to the right. The area to the bottom right is now the site of the nuclear power station. *(British Railways)*

A 'Black Five' heads past Torrisholme No. 1 Junction with a Morecambe to Leeds express in August 1964.
(Peter Sunderland)

Electric unit No. 28219 takes the curve into Morecambe at Torrisholme No. 2 Junction in August 1964.
(Peter Sunderland)

Electrification

One of the four Midland power cars inside Heysham Station about 1920. *(British Railways)*

The local service between Lancaster, Morecambe and Heysham was operated by two steam railcars. These were the only ones used on the Midland Railway, having been built specially for this line. Numbered 2233 and 2234, each was 60ft long with separate passenger and luggage compartments, the latter totally enclosing the engine. They had a short working life because in 1906 it was decided to electrify from Lancaster to Morecambe and Heysham as an experiment in what the chairman called 'the motive power of the future'. The company may well have selected this outpost for the experiment to avoid the risk of teething troubles on a busier commuter route. There was also the advantage of the existing railway owned power station at Heysham which supplied the cranes and other dock facilities.

Traction current was at 6,600 volts a.c. from overhead wires. Rolling stock comprised three power cars and four driving trailers. This allowed the making up of two 3 coach trains with a power car spare. The service was inaugurated in sections: from Heysham to Morecambe on 13 April 1908, to Lancaster Green Ayre on 1 July and to Castle Station on 14 September.

The timetable was somewhat erratic but the electric trains combined with the longer distance steam trains to give 28 departures each weekday from Lancaster Green Ayre to Morecambe. A handful came through from Lancaster Castle. There were ten workings a day between Morecambe and Heysham. The electric trains did not run on Sundays at that time.

The Midland electric stock lasted until 11 February 1951. The following day, a steam push-pull service took over. This employed Stanier 0-4-4 tanks numbered 41900 to 41904 which had been kept in store awaiting this eventuality.

The electrification equipment was then converted from single phase 25 cycles a.c. to 50 cycles. The 6,600 voltage was retained. 'New' rolling stock was introduced comprising three-car trains built in 1914 for the Willesden-Earls Court service of the London & North Western Railway. This service had been withdrawn in 1940 but the trains had been stored. They were converted from third rail d.c. to overhead a.c. and refurbished internally with the 'bus type' seats which became familiar on diesel multiple units throughout BR. They began making trial runs from 11 November 1952 and took

Steam railcar and trailer at Heysham pre electrification.
(Lancaster City Museum)

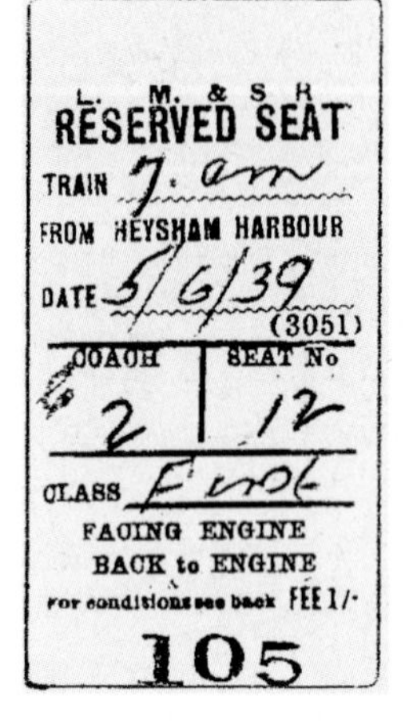

L. M. & S. R.
RESERVED SEAT
TRAIN 7. am
FROM HEYSHAM HARBOUR
DATE 5/6/39
(3051)

COACH	SEAT No
2	12

CLASS First
FACING ENGINE
BACK to ENGINE
For conditions see back FEE 1/-
105

LMS No. 28611, one of the Midland power cars arriving at Morecambe Promenade about 1946 with an ordinary coach converted for use as driving trailer. The board beneath the pantograph reads 'It is dangerous to touch this apparatus'.
(W. Hubert Foster, courtesy John Holroyd)

LMS No 29292, one of the original driving trailer coaches.
(W. Hubert Foster, courtesy John Holroyd)

over the full service on 17 August 1953.

The electric trains were suspended for further experiments between October 1955 and March 1956 when a new type of on board rectifier was fitted to convert the a.c. supply to the d.c. traction motors. Although the relatively low 6,600 voltage was retained, this was the proving ground for the subsequent standard British electrification at 25,000 volts a.c.

An intermediate station was opened at Scale Hall on 8 June 1957. At that time there was a basic half hourly electric service from Morecambe via Green Ayre to Lancaster Castle. On weekdays this ran from 6.10am to 11.10pm. The service from Heysham was more erratic with 13 electric departures each weekday. There were also the boat trains from Heysham and the Leeds trains between Morecambe and Lancaster Green Ayre.

On Sundays, the local service ran only between mid April and the end of October with a half hourly departure from Morecambe Promenade to Lancaster Castle between 12.10 and 11.10pm. There were no electric trains to Heysham on Sundays.

After the withdrawal of the boat trains in 1975, the Heysham branch relied on traffic from the ICI works served by a branch from Heysham Moss. Here there were extensive sidings controlled from a standard LMS flat roof signal box. The whole complex was built at the start of the Second World War.

Traffic from this source had dried up by 1986 when the nuclear power station opened. This is adjacent to Heysham station and sees traffic about once a week to Sellafield. Passenger trains resumed on 11 May 1987 to connect with the Isle of Man sailing.

In 1994, the track layout was rationalised in connection with the replacement station at Morecambe. Heysham Moss signal box was abolished and the entire branch reduced to a single line, controlled by a staff which is issued to the driver at Bare Lane. From here to Morecambe the double track is worked as two single lines. The one on the north side leads only into platform 1 at Morecambe station and is worked without a token. The other one leads into platform 2 where there is a loco run round loop. Trains for Heysham must reverse direction in platform 2.

The point giving access to the branch is operated by the guard using the single line staff as the key to unlock the ground frame.

A Lancaster to Morecambe electric coasts into Scale Hall on 6 August 1961.
(Geoffrey Lewthwaite)

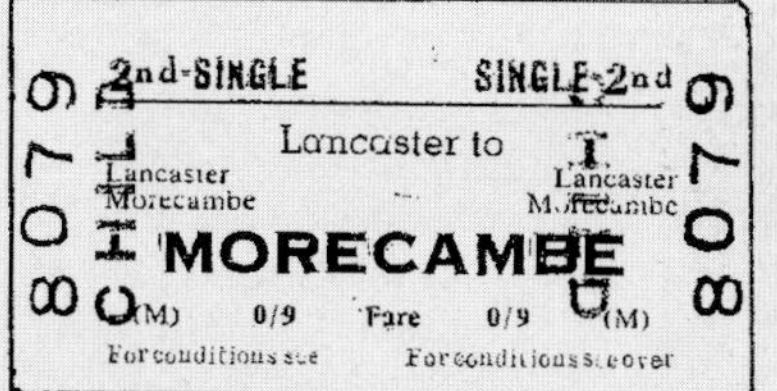

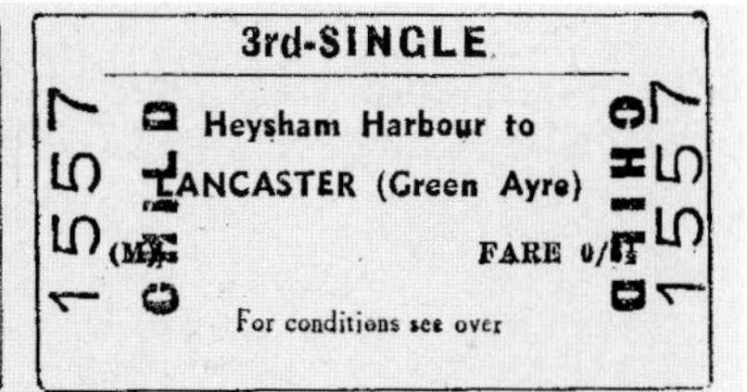

Lying derelict at Green Ayre shed in July 1960 is Stanier 0-4-4T No. 41904, one of the push-pull fitted locos used to cover for the electric service in 1951-53 and 1955-56.
(Peter Sunderland)

Two of the ex LNWR three car sets, driving trailers leading, at Morecambe Promenade in May 1958.
(Peter Sunderland)

An electric unit descending from Lancaster Castle towards Green Ayre in July 1960.
(Peter Sunderland)

Electric unit for Heysham in platform 5 at Lancaster Castle on 24 September 1963. *(Peter E. Baughan)*

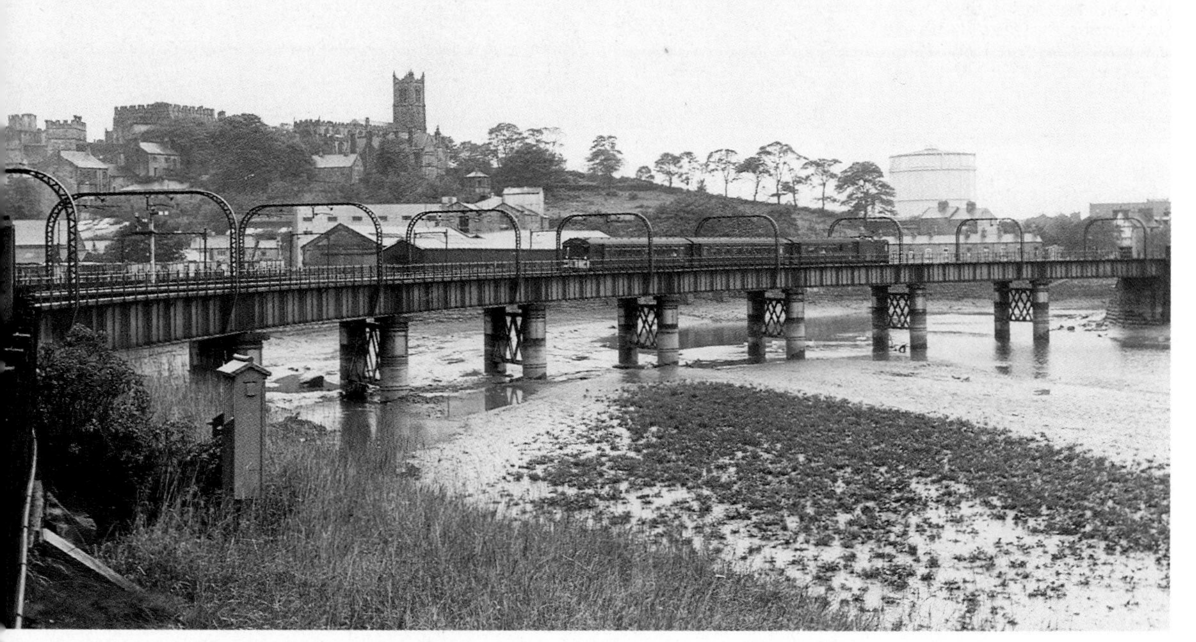
The Midland Lune Viaduct or Greyhound Bridge with an electric unit from Morecambe approaching Lancaster Green Ayre on 24 September 1963. *(Peter E. Baughan)*

28220 leaving Lancaster Castle for Morecambe Promenade, June 1958.
(Peter Sunderland)

A Morecambe to Heysham working at Torrisholme No. 2 Junction. The direct Lancaster to Heysham line is to the right.
(Peter Sunderland)

A Morecambe to Lancaster electric about to pass under the Carlisle Bridge as a local passenger train heads towards Carnforth in 1962. The bridge was rebuilt during the following year hence the scaffolding.
(Peter Sunderland)

Closure and Diversions

No longer a junction, 40169 approaching Wennington with the Heysham to Haverton Hill ammonia tanks on 27 March 1982. *(Tom Heavyside)*

By the early 1960s it would have come as little surprise had BR announced closure, at least to passengers, of the ex LNWR Morecambe branch and the ex Furness & Midland between Wennington and Carnforth.

In the former case, the only passengers dependant upon the service were commuters from Bare Lane into Lancaster. In the latter case, the intermediate stations had all closed. The only significant traffic was in passengers seeking connections at Carnforth with either the Furness or West Coast Main Line. It required a double change, at Green Ayre and Castle Stations, to effect a connection in Lancaster.

The Beeching Report recommended the opposite to the above. It proposed closure of the Lancaster, Morecambe & Heysham electrics together with the former Midland route from Wennington to Morecambe. It also threatened closure of every intermediate station between Skipton and Carnforth. The service from Leeds to Morecambe and Heysham (via Carnforth) was listed as one 'to be modified'.

A proposal to close the electric service and divert Leeds–Morecambe trains via Carnforth was put through the statutory TUCC procedure in 1965. The latter body reported that little hardship would ensue and the last electric trains ran on Saturday 1 January 1966. There was no electric service on a winter Sunday but the last Leeds–Morecambe trains via Lancaster Green Ayre ran on 2 January. From the next day, the practice of splitting trains at Wennington was dispensed with as all took the F&M route to Carnforth whence they proceeded via the Hest Bank to Bare Lane curve to reach Morecambe Promenade. They stopped at Bare Lane which also gained from an enhanced Lancaster Castle to Morecambe service offered as a replacement to the withdrawn electrics. All services were dmu operated. In fact most Leeds-Morecambe trains had changed from steam or diesel haulage to dmu the previous March when units became spare on the withdrawal of some local services in Airedale and Wharfedale. For the intervening nine months, dmus had been splitting at Wennington for Morecambe and Carnforth.

The British Railways Act 1965 had authorised construction of a curve just outside Morecambe which would have given direct access from Bare Lane towards Heysham. This would have permitted closure of Morecambe Promenade and the reopening of Euston Road which was nearer the town centre. But it never happened.

From the point of view of passengers, the worst consequence of the closure and diversion was that

28219 waits departure from Morecambe Promenade for Heysham on 23 May 1964. The electric service was a victim of the diversion. *(Martin Bairstow Collection)*

45428, now preserved, approaching Carnforth with a Morecambe to Leeds Saturday extra on 26 August 1967. This was the last summer with even occasional steam on the passenger service.

(Tom Heavyside)

The diverted Leeds-Morecambe trains did not stop at Hest Bank which closed on 4 November 1967. Fairburn tank No. 42135 arrives with a train for Lancaster on 6 August 1961. *(Geoffrey Lewthwaite)*

Lancaster Green Ayre, July 1960 with an electric from Morecambe to Lancaster Castle reversing in the platform. *(Peter Sunderland)*

Lancaster Castle is not as convenient for the City Centre as was Green Ayre. Fowler 2-6-4T No. 42322 has brought a local, possibly a Barrow-Preston, into Lancaster Castle on 24 September 1963. *(Peter E. Baughan)*

Leeds–Morecambe trains no longer served Lancaster.

From the freight angle, this didn't matter. Traffic from the 'Little' North Western towards Barrow was much better going via the Furness & Midland than the alternative of negotiating the incline from Green Ayre to Lancaster Castle where run round would have been necessary. Traffic from Leeds to Heysham could also be worked equally well via Carnforth especially if the Morecambe curve had been built.

One can only assume that freight was thought to be the more important consideration at least in the short term. Perhaps BR didn't intend there to be a long term for the 'Little' North Western. They cannot have foreseen that 35 years later, freight has disappeared totally from the routes in question yet the passenger service has survived.

They never took any step to close the seven intermediate stations between Skipton and Carnforth. What they did do, in 1970, was close the main line platforms at Carnforth. This destroyed any chance of passengers connecting from Leeds to Windermere or the North.

In 1982, BR reduced the service over the Settle & Carlisle Line. As an alternative they offered three Leeds–Glasgow connections at Lancaster. To achieve this, they accelerated three out of the seven Leeds–Morecambe trains to run non stop from Skipton to Carnforth. These trains then ran via Lancaster giving an overall Leeds–Morecambe time about the same as the direct stopping trains. Glasgow passengers found themselves passing through Carnforth twice. The three Leeds–Lancaster–Morecambe trains were worked by four car hybrid dmus created by amalgamating parts of 'Trans Pennine' and Swindon Cross Country sets.

By 1987, the Settle & Carlisle service had been improved and few journeys were being made changing at Lancaster. It had, however, been discovered that Lancaster was an important traffic centre in its own right.

From 1984 the three Leeds–Morecambe 'express' dmus were replaced by class 31 loco hauled trains which ran only as far as Lancaster. Rather than run the locomotive round to go to Morecambe, they offered a dmu connection.

In 1987 class 142 and 144 'pacer' dmus took over services in Airedale and Wharfedale including workings to Lancaster and Morecambe, most of which became extensions of Leeds–Skipton stopping trains. All trains ran via Lancaster to Morecambe taking around 2 hours 20 minutes for the overall journey, most calling at all stations.

In October 1990, the number of Leeds–Lancaster trains was reduced to four a day with through workings to Morecambe only on summer Saturdays and Sundays. Most stopped at all stations between Leeds and Skipton. A measure of improvement came in September 1995 when electrification was completed in Airedale and Wharfedale. Since then there have been four trains each weekday through from Leeds to Morecambe via Lancaster plus an early morning working between Skipton and Lancaster only. Between Leeds and Skipton, the Morecambe trains are quite separate from the half hourly locals. Most stop only at Shipley and Keighley. Some are worked by class 156, 'sprinters' in preference to the four wheel 'pacers'. On Sundays there are four trains from Leeds to Morecambe but the two morning ones run only from April until September.

52087 leads a hybrid Trans Pennine/Swindon Cross Country set on the 17.12 Leeds–Morecambe. It is restarting from Lancaster on 29 May 1982. *(Tom Heavyside)*

'Britannia' 4-6-0 No. 70010 'Owen Glendower' passing Hest Bank with two parcels vans in August 1967. *(Tom Heavyside)*

Still with a first class section, 50271 leads a 3 car Metro Cammell set, leaving Bentham for Leeds on 12 December 1981. *(Tom Heavyside)*

A Morecambe to Leeds dmu pulls away from Giggleswick on 1 September 1975. The 'bus shelter' is about to replace the station building. *(Alan Young)*

A four car dmu crossing Clapham Viaduct en route from Leeds to Morecambe on 19 January 1980. *(Tom Heavyside)*

A new use for the Wennington to Morecambe Line

Following closure to passengers, the line between Wennington, Lancaster and Morecambe remained open as a through route for freight until 3 June 1967. After this, two short sections were worked as sidings. Until 31 January 1970, the North Western Gas Board sidings at White Lund were served from the Morecambe direction. Initially the line remained double but from 23 October 1967, White Lund was accessible only by a single track from Torrisholme No 2 Junction (on the Heysham branch). Morecambe to Torrisholme No 1 was closed.

Until March 1976, a single track ran from Lancaster Castle through the remains of Green Ayre as far as the power station at Ladies Walk. The Greyhound Bridge, the viaduct over the Lune near Green Ayre, was converted into a road. This created a level crossing with the surviving goods line at Green Ayre until 1976.

The disused track bed from Morecambe to the Greyhound Bridge, the Torrisholme curve, the Lancaster Castle branch, and the main line to beyond Caton were bought by the local authority for use as a footpath and cycle way. Between Morecambe and Lancaster it is surfaced with tarmac and equipped with lighting. East of Lancaster, it is being brought up to a similar standard.

The path begins alongside Morecambe station running alongside the railway until it crosses the Heysham branch. Then it assumes the track bed. At the other end, there is a car park and picnic site at Bull Beck, about 1/2 mile east of Caton, where you can join the path which actually extends a further 1/4 mile eastward to the point where the River Lune is adjacent. From here suitably clad walkers, but not cyclists, may continue towards Hornby on a riverside path except that this is temporarily blocked by erosion of the river bank. The local authority is hoping to by-pass the obstruction.

The former Midland cycle path almost connects with the ex LNWR branch from Lancaster to Glasson Dock. Opened in 1883, this closed to passengers in 1930 and to goods in 1964. It is now a footpath/cycle way for most of its 5 1/2 mile length running alongside the Lune estuary for much of the way.

Adrian not exactly speeding across the west viaduct at Crook O'Lune in May 2000. He is heading towards Halton. *(John Holroyd)*

Halton Station is well preserved as a boat house for a local rowing club. *(Martin Bairstow)*

The former station at Bell Busk, now used as a restaurant, photographed from a passing train in 1974. *(Alan Young)*

42484 in the bay at Hellifield, ready to depart with the last train to Hawes on 7 March 1959. *(Geoffrey Lewthwaite)*

144007 calls at Giggleswick, Morecambe bound, on 1 July 1989. As predicted on page 70, the 'bus shelter' has indeed become the Main Station building. *(Martin Bairstow)*

Heysham For Ireland

The 'Londonderry' arriving Heysham soon after entering service in 1904. Behind is sister ship 'Donegal' which was sunk in 1917. *(British Railways)*

Three new ships were ordered by the Midland Railway for the Heysham to Belfast service. 'Antrim' and 'Donegal' were twin screw steamships of 2,100 gross tons. 'Londonderry' was a triple screw turbine steamer.

'Antrim' inaugurated the service from Heysham to Belfast on 1 September 1904, sailing at 11pm following arrival of the Boat Train which had left London St Pancras at 5pm via Leeds. 'Londonderry' provided the corresponding 9pm departure from Belfast overnight to Heysham with onward train connection to Leeds and London where St Pancras station was reached at 11.20am.

Laird Line transferred its business from Morecambe to Heysham where it was offered use of a berth 'in perpetuity'. Laird Line advertised its Dublin and Londonderry sailings 'in direct connection with Midland through Express Trains which arrive and depart alongside the steamer'. Departures for Dublin North Wall were at 9pm daily except Sundays. On Tuesdays and Saturdays, there was a sailing, also at 9pm, for Londonderry.

Services were interrupted during the First World War but resumed afterwards. By summer 1922, the Heysham to Dublin timetable was identical to pre war. The times to Londonderry had changed but sailings were still twice weekly. The Dublin sailings ceased in 1926, possibly because the LMS wanted the berth and was willing to pay compensation for breaching the 1904 agreement. The Londonderry route ceased to carry passengers about 1936 but survived for freight and cattle until October 1963. Laird Line had been part of Burns & Laird since 1922.

The LMS reorganised its Irish Sea shipping in 1928, closing the Fleetwood to Belfast route and diverting London and Manchester boat trains to Heysham. These ran by the LNWR main line to Lancaster Castle then via Bare Lane to Morecambe Promenade where they had to reverse direction.

The decision in favour of Heysham was based in part by the amount of dredging which would have been required to keep fixed timetables at Fleetwood, especially with larger ships.

Three new vessels were provided for the Heysham to Belfast route in 1928. The 'Duke of Lancaster', 'Duke of Rothesay' and 'Duke of Argyll' were each 3,600 ton twin funnelled turbine steamers. They maintained a nightly service with daytime crossings scheduled only on peak summer Saturdays.

One entry in the timetable could represent two or even more ships as relief sailings were operated at busy times. As an example, on Friday 4 August 1939, the eve of a bank holiday weekend, four ships left Heysham.

	Departed	No. of Passengers first class	third class
Princess Margaret	11.28 pm	139	1,388
Duke of York	12.08 am	104	1,396
Duke of Lancaster	12.59 am	250	572
Duke of Rothesay	1.03 am	229	791
		722	4,147

A total of 4,869 passengers, most of whom would have reached Heysham by connecting trains.

The 'Duke of York' was built in 1935 as relief ship for this route with high capacity for steerage (third class) passengers. It also made cargo only crossings with the passenger accommodation closed off. The 'Princess Margaret' was a visitor from the Stranraer– Larne route. At that time, Northern Ireland was a popular tourist destination enthusiastically promoted by the LMS Railway which ran most of the cross channel ships and many of the trains in Northern Ireland itself.

Many of the railway steamers were requisitioned during the Second World War. The Heysham to Belfast Service was maintained except between April and August 1944 when the ships were all called up for D Day. The ships employed during the War years were not necessarily the regular steamers nor even railway owned vessels.

The November 1944 *Bradshaw* does not give the times of ships for obvious security reasons but it does show the Heysham boat trains running three days per week. This implies that the ship was sailing from Belfast on Monday, Wednesday and Friday nights returning from Heysham overnight on Tuesday, Thursday and Saturday.

Heysham was a restricted area during the War and *Bradshaw* shows no local electric trains from Morecambe. These must actually have been running for workmen.

The winter 1948/49 timetable shows the normal nightly service leaving Belfast at 9.40pm, arriving Heysham at 5.00am. Connecting trains then depart as follows:

Duke of Lancaster, Duke of Argyll, Duke of Rothesay

THE SERVICES
WITH
NORTHERN IRELAND

Commencing 30th April, 1928

		Mondays to Fridays. p.m.	p.m.	Saturdays. p.m.	p.m.
LONDON (Euston)	leave	6.10	—	6.40	—
(St. Pancras)	,,	—	5.0	—	5. 0
BIRMINGHAM (New St.) ...	,,	5.50	—	[illegible]	—
CREWE	,,	8.10	—	9.40	—
NOTTINGHAM	,,	The	7.22	The	7.22
SHEFFIELD	,,	Ulster	8.34	Ulster	8.34
LEEDS (Wellington) ...	,,	Express	9.30	Express	9.30
BRADFORD (Forster Square)	,,	—	9. 0	—	9. 0
MANCHESTER (Victoria)...	,,	—	9. 5	—	9. 5
PRESTON	,,	10.14	—	10.44	—
HEYSHAM	arrive	11. 1	11.25	11.33	11.25
... ...	leave	11.50		11.50	
BELFAST	arrive	6.30 a.m.		6.30 a.m.	

Passengers to England leave Belfast at 9.15 p.m. Mondays to Fridays, and at 11.0 p.m. on Saturdays, and there are Express Train connections at Heysham to London and the Provinces.

Full details of services and Tourist, Week-end and Excursion Fares between England and Ireland (via Holyhead, Heysham and Stranraer), may be obtained at L M S Stations and Offices.

IRELAND BY L M S

Four LMS vessels at Heysham on 4 August 1939, preparing for the overnight crossing to Belfast. From the right: 'Princess Margaret', 'Duke of Lancaster', 'Duke of York', 'Duke of Rothesay'. The fifth vessel, facing the other way, is the 'Snaefell' of the Isle of Man Steam Packet Company. *(Gordon Fairbanks)*

5.55 Hellifield, Skipton, Keighley, Bingley, Leeds City.
6.10 Morecambe Prom, Chorley (by request to set down from Belfast), Bolton, Salford, Manchester Victoria.
6.30 Morecambe Prom, Crewe, London Euston.
7.12 (electric) Morecambe Prom, Lancaster GA, Lancaster Castle. (This connected at Morecambe with the 'residential' to Bradford and Leeds).
7.40 Lancaster GA, all stations to Skipton, Keighley, Bingley, Leeds. (This was a boat train for people who enjoyed more of a lie in).

In the other direction, the ship left Heysham at 11.40pm after connecting trains had arrived from London, Manchester and Leeds at 10.06, 10.59 and 11.21pm respectively. The service ran six days per week. There was no sailing on Sunday night.

The three 'Dukes' dating from 1928 were replaced in 1956 by new 4,500 ton vessels bearing the same names. In 1958 a BR container service was introduced between Heysham and Belfast with two purpose built ships 'Container Enterprise' and 'Container Venturer'.

The 'Duke of Rothesay' reversing into Heysham about 1933. *(British Railways)*

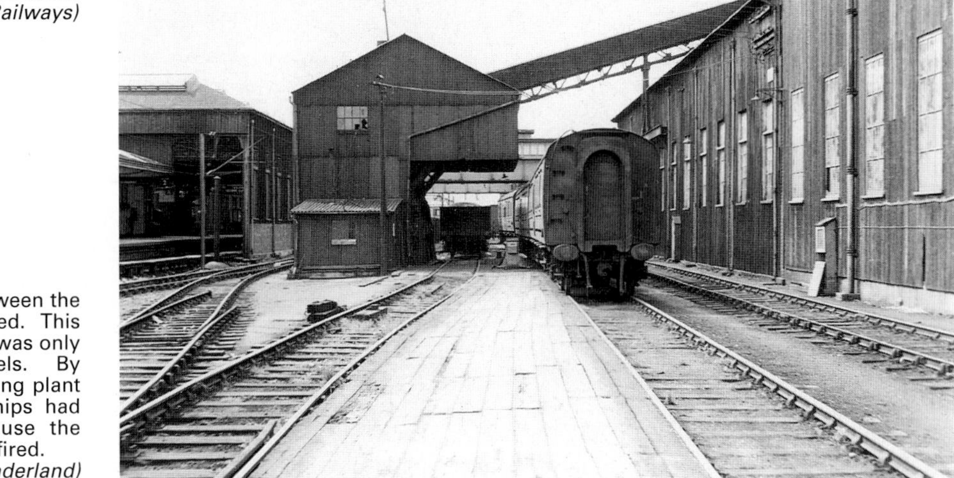

The coaling plant between the station and transit shed. This remaining apparatus was only for the freight vessels. By 1959, the corresponding plant for the passenger ships had been removed because the new vessels were oil fired. *(Peter Sunderland)*

On board 'Slieve Bawn' in Heysham Harbour, 1949. Newly built 2-6-4T No. 52 is on its way from Derby Works to Belfast for the Northern Counties Committee. *(Peter Sunderland)*

The 'Duke of Argyll' and 'Slieve Bawn' at Heysham in April 1960. *(British Railways)*

JULY ISSUE.—New and Improved Travel Facilities. D 1798

LMS London Midland & Scottish Railway **LMS**

HOLIDAY RETURN TICKETS, 1931

FRIDAYS & †SATURDAYS, July 24th to Oct. 31st

TO THE

NORTH OF IRELAND

(VIA HEYSHAM and BELFAST).

Also SATURDAYS, July 25th to October 31st, inclusive

To LONDONDERRY

(VIA HEYSHAM and Direct Steamer).

FROM	TIMES OF DEPARTURE.		
	Fridays, July 24 to Aug. 14.	Fridays, Aug. 21 to Oct. 30, Saturdays all dates.	Sats. to Londonderry only via Heysham and Direct Steamer.
NORMANTON	8 39 p.m.	8 39 p.m.	8 39 p.m.
WOODLESFORD	8 53 „	8 53 „	8 53 „
LEEDS (Wellington)	9 35 „	9 30 „	9 30 „
ARMLEY	8 44 „	8 44 „	8 44 „
KIRKSTALL	8 48 „	8 48 „	8 48 „
NEWLAY	8 53 „	8 53 „	8 53 „
CALVERLEY	8 57 „	8 57 „	8 57 „
APPERLEY	9 2 „	9 2 „	9 2 „
BRADFORD (Forster Square)	9A40 „	9A 0 „	9 0 „
MANNINGHAM	9A 9 „	9A 5 „	9 5 „
FRIZINGHALL	9A12 „	9A 8 „	9 8 „
SHIPLEY	9A55 „	9A14 „	9 14 „
ILKLEY	8*29 „	8*29 „	8*29 „
BEN RHYDDING	8*32 „	8*30 „	8*30 „
BURLEY	8*37 „	8*35 „	8*35 „
OTLEY	7*34 „	7*34 „	7*34 „
MENSTON	8*42 „	8*42 „	8*42 „
GUISELEY	8*49 „	8*49 „	8*49 „
HEYSHAM (for Belfast) ... dep. about	11 50 „	11 40 „	—
HEYSHAM (for Londonderry) „ „			11 45 „

* Change at Shipley. A—Friday and Saturday, August 7th and 8th, excepted—see special handbills for Bradford Holidays.

OUTWARD ARRANGEMENTS.

Passengers for Londonderry (direct Steamer) leave Heysham about 11.45 p.m. on Saturday, and arrive at Londonderry about 3.0 p.m. Sunday. Passengers on Fridays and Saturdays for Belfast and Interior Stations leave Heysham at 11.40 p.m., and are due to arrive at BELFAST (Donegall Quay) about 6.30 a.m. on Saturdays and Sundays. Those for Interior Stations travel by first train after arrival. Passengers for Stations marked A go forward from Belfast (York Road) Station. Passengers for Stations marked B go forward from Belfast (Gt. Victoria St.) Station. Passengers for Stations marked C go forward from Belfast (Queen's Quay) Station.

†—SPECIAL NOTE.—Passengers booking to Irish interior stations on Saturdays must ascertain before commencing the journey that there is a through service to their destination.

RETURN ARRANGEMENTS.

Passengers RETURN ANY SAILING DAY within 16 days from and including date of outward journey as follows :—

HEYSHAM-BELFAST SERVICE.

By Ordinary Train to join Steamer leaving Belfast at 9.15 p.m. Sundays to Fridays, and 11.0 p.m. Saturdays, except on Fridays, July 24th to September 4th, inclusive.

Each Saturday, July 25th to September 5th, inclusive, a Special Steamer giving a Daylight Sailing will leave Belfast at 10.0 a.m., due Heysham about 5.0 p.m., and, except those from the places mentioned in the succeeding paragraph, all returning excursion passengers will require to travel by this Saturday morning service from Belfast, and will not be permitted to travel by the Friday night sailing during the period the Saturday morning service is in force.

Return Excursion Passengers from the following places, viz. :—

Ballycastle. Coleraine. Killybegs. Londonderry.
Ballymoney. Donegal. Letterkenny. Portrush.
Bundoran. Giant's Causeway. Limavady. Portstewart.
Castlerock. Glenties.

will require to make use of the night service from Belfast, owing to there being no train service into Belfast on the Saturday morning to connect with a 10.0 a.m. steamer departure.

LONDONDERRY (Direct Steamer) SERVICE.

Passengers from LONDONDERRY (Direct Steamer) return from Prince's Quay on either Mondays (except August 3rd) at 4.30 p.m., or Fridays at 12.0 noon (no return later than Friday week following date of outward journey), going forward from Heysham by first connecting train.

Passengers are requested to obtain their tickets in advance as this will assist the Company in the provision of accommodation.

Tickets can be purchased at the COMPANY'S STATIONS; or at the OFFICES of THOS. COOK & SON, LTD., 55, Boar Lane, LEEDS, and 21, Market Street, BRADFORD; and from Messrs. A. ALTHAM, LTD., 4, New Market Street, 255, Hunslet Road, and 34a, Tong Road, LEEDS; and 21, Westgate, and 140, Manchester Road, BRADFORD; and from the BRADFORD CO-OPERATIVE SOCIETY, 65, Sunbridge Road, BRADFORD; from the WINDHILL CO-OPERATIVE SOCIETY, Market Place, SHIPLEY; and Messrs. TRAVELLERS LIMITED, 5, Boar Lane, LEEDS.

The advent of car ferries

The 1960s saw an increase in tourist traffic to Northern Ireland but many passengers wanted to take their own cars. 'The Duke of Rothesay' was withdrawn in 1966 for conversion to a car ferry for the Fishguard to Rosslare route.

During the winter of 1969/70, the other two 'Dukes' were similarly converted in anticipation of turning Heysham–Belfast into a car ferry operation from May 1970. A link span was built at the east end of the south quay. About the same time, the railway station was moved a little to the east, the Midland's wooden island platform giving way to a new three platform structure which opened on 4 May 1970.

Heysham to Dun Laoghaire

In June 1970 a summer only thrice weekly car ferry was introduced between Heysham and Dun Laoghaire employing a vessel based at Holyhead. It had not been pre-planned that Heysham should also have a nightly passenger sailing to Dun Laoghaire but on 23 May 1970, two youths managed to set fire to the Britannia Tubular Bridge which carried the railway from the Welsh mainland onto Anglesey (see *The North Wales Coast Railway*). From 25 May, the 'Irish Mail' rail/sea service between London and Dun Laoghaire was diverted via Heysham. This arrangement lasted for 20 months whilst the Britannia Bridge was under repair. The last 'mail boat' left Heysham on 30 January 1972. This was the final Dun Laoghaire sailing from Heysham. The car ferry, which was quite independent of the 'mail' service, had not been judged a success. It had run only during the 1970 and 1971 seasons, making its last crossing on 18 September 1971.

Heysham Harbour 16 August 1970. The 'Duke of Lancaster' (left) is on the car ferry link span. The 'St. David' (centre) and 'Hibernia' are here thanks to the diversion of Dun Laoghaire traffic.

(Peter Sunderland)

The tug/tender 'Wyvern' served at Heysham from 1904 until 1959. In its early days, it held a passenger certificate in order to work from Heysham to Fleetwood.
(Peter Sunderland Collection)

The 'Dover' on the linkspan adjacent to the then new Heysham Station working the Dun Laoghaire car ferry on 23 July 1970.
(Peter Sunderland)

'Duke of Argyll' leaving Heysham for Belfast on 27 July 1971. 'Hibernia' is on the diverted Dun Laoghaire service. *(Peter Sunderland)*

Part of the BR Cargo fleet, 'Container Venturer' moored alongside 'Slieve Bearnagh' at Heysham about 1965.
(F.W. Smith Collection)

'Duke of Argyll' and 'Slieve Bearnagh' at Belfast Donegall Quay in August 1959. Built in 1936 for the freight and livestock businesses, 'Slieve Bearnagh' and sister ship 'Slieve Bawn' made their last crossings in December 1971.
(Peter Sunderland)

Closure

By 1974, the Heysham to Belfast service was in difficulty. Tourist traffic to Northern Ireland had been killed off by civil unrest whilst many commercial freight carriers had been attracted to the purpose built lorry ferries operated by P&O from Fleetwood.

British Railways published a formal closure proposal which had to go through the same TUCC procedure as a railway closure. A public hearing was duly held in Morecambe prior to the Minister of Transport giving his consent to the closure. The last sailings took place on the night of 5/6 April 1975. BR then went through the same closure procedure in respect of the connecting trains. For the next six months, one of the 'boat trains' still ran until formal consent was obtained to close the Morecambe–Heysham branch to passengers from 6 October 1975.

The 'Duke of Argyll' was sold to the Mediterranean. After a spell on the Fishguard to Rosslare service, the 'Duke of Lancaster' was sold to become a floating restaurant on the North Wales Coast. The project failed but, still in 1999, the derelict ship can be seen beached alongside the railway between Holywell Junction and Mostyn.

From 1975, the level of shipping activity at Heysham was down to little more than the Belfast container service. From 1978 this became an entirely roll on-roll off operation.

The 'Duke of Argyll' leaving Heysham for Belfast in July 1967. As the 'Corinthia', it sailed on in Greek waters until the early 1990s becoming the last turbine steamer in the Mediterranean. *(Peter Sunderland)*

'Sea Cat Danmark' reversing into the berth alongside Heysham Station upon arrival from Belfast in August 1999. To the right is the 'Lady of Mann'. *(Stuart Baker)*

Revival

The fortunes of Heysham began to improve when James Fisher & Sons Ltd opened a warehouse for fruit imported from the Mediterranean on the site of the old passenger station. Then came the revived Isle of Man service in 1978, which led eventually to the reinstated passenger train in 1987. These developments appear in the next chapter.

In 1984 Heysham was among the railway ports sold to Sea Containers. On 30 March 1999, this organisation reintroduced a passenger and a car ferry service to Belfast. It is a very different operation to its predecessor of 1904-1975 being handled by a high speed catamaran which completes its four hour crossing in day time. The service was suspended during January, February and March 2000 but resumed in April with a departure daily at 7.00 from Belfast returning from Heysham at 12.00. On most days, there is a second crossing at 17.30 from Belfast and 22.15 from Heysham. A morning train connection was introduced from 29 May 2000. The evening sailing has a bus to and from Lancaster Station.

Passenger/car ferries leave from the link span adjacent to the railway station. There are two other link spans which are used by roll on-roll off freight vessels to Ireland. There are four sailings per day to Belfast, two to Warrenpoint and two to Dublin. These run exclusively for the road haulage industry. They merit reference in a railway book because, together with the passenger/car ferries, they have brought new life to the former Midland Railway port of Heysham.

Registered in La Spezia and flying the Italian flag, 'Superseacat Two' leaves Heysham for Belfast in May 2000. *(Martin Bairstow)*

'Sea Cat Danmark' worked the Belfast service in 1999. It will return to Heysham on peak days during 2000 to augment the Isle of Man sailings. *(Stuart Baker)*

Heysham for the Isle of Man

The 'Manxman' at Heysham before the First World War. *(British Railways)*

On 1 June 1905, the Midland Railway began a summer only service between Heysham and Douglas employing the 2,174 ton 'Manxman'. Built by Vickers at Barrow, the triple screw 'Manxman' was one of the largest and fastest cross channel ferries of its time. With a service speed of 22½ knots, it could accommodate 1,600 passengers who were afforded 'ample scope for exercise' on three decks. The dining room seated 100 people whilst the 'magnificent smoke room with an arched roof 14 feet high is provided with all the comforts conducive to contemplative ease. There is no second class, but the third class accommodation is equal to the second class usually allotted in vessels of this kind'.

The ship left Douglas at 9.15am returning from Heysham at 2.35pm. Journey time was three hours. It was laid up after 5 October 1905 but returned on 21 May 1906 to work a more ambitious timetable, aided by other vessels, of up to three return sailings per day.

The Isle of Man Steam Packet felt the effect of competition from the 'Manxman' particularly on their Fleetwood to Douglas route. They retaliated by ordering their first turbine steamer, the 'Viking' but the Midland Railway replied by offering a connecting service from Fleetwood to Douglas via Heysham using their steam tug/passenger tender 'Wyvern' for the 40 minute crossing from Fleetwood to Heysham.

The Heysham to Douglas service was suspended at the start of the First World War when the 'Manxman' was first requisitioned and later purchased by the Admiralty for conversion into a sea plane carrier. It survived the war but the Midland Railway declined to buy it back. Instead, it went to the Isle of Man Steam Packet in 1920.

The Midland Railway resumed the summer service between Heysham and Douglas in 1920. *Bradshaw* for July 1922 shows the 'Isle of Man Boat Express' leaving both Leeds Wellington and Bradford Market Street each weekday at 7.17am, joining up at Shipley, then calling at Bingley, Keighley, Skipton and Lancaster Green Ayre to arrive Heysham at 9.40am. Departure time of the ship is not shown but arrival in Douglas is advertised at 2pm. The return is at 4pm from Douglas with the boat train leaving Heysham at 8.25 for Leeds and Bradford. It looks as though the ships then in use were allowed four hours for the crossing. The 'Manxman' had achieved a record run of two hours 30 minutes in August 1909.

In 1928, the LMS rationalised its Irish Sea services, ceding the Heysham–Douglas route and two ships to the Isle of Man Steam Packet. 'Antrim' became 'Ramsey Town' and 'Duke of Cornwall' ecame 'Rushen Castle' in the Manx fleet.

The July 1938 *Bradshaw* shows a daily service except Sundays) at 10am from Heysham, 4pm from)ouglas with train connections from Leeds and 3radford. There was an extra service on Saturdays, n extra two on peak summer Saturdays, also with rain connections.

The service was suspended again at the outbreak of the Second World War. Most of the Steam Packet leet was requisitioned. Three of them were lost on he same day at Dunkirk. The 'Manxman' survived)unkirk to become 'HMS Caduceus'. After lecommissioning in 1945, it regained its old name nd ferried troops and prisoners of war, mainly etween Harwich and the Hook of Holland. It was old for scrap in 1949.

The Steam Packet did not resume seasonal ailings between Heysham and Douglas until 1953 nd then only on a very limited basis with no more han a dozen sailings per year, all of them midweek n July and August. After Heysham lost the electric rains in 1966, a special dmu was run from Lancaster nd Morecambe on the odd days that the ship sailed.

'Mona's Isle' worked the last Douglas to leysham sailing on 28 August 1974. The Steam 'acket blamed higher oil prices and reduced atronage together with the impending closure by 3ritish Railways of their remaining passenger ervices, rail and ship, from Heysham.

Manx Line

In 1978, the Isle of Man Steam Packet still ran eight ships: four side loading car ferries, two traditional passenger steamers and two freight vessels. With this fleet they offered separate daily services for cars/passengers and for freight between Liverpool and Douglas. They also managed seasonal sailings to Douglas, no more than two or three times a week, from each of Fleetwood, Llandudno, Dublin, Belfast and Ardrossan. Half the ships spent eight months of the year laid up. The roll on-roll off revolution had so far bypassed the Isle of Man. The Steam Packet appeared most reluctant to embrace it.

Manx Line was promoted to offer a multi purpose roll on-roll off service between Heysham and Douglas. Much to the annoyance of the Steam Packet, the Isle of Man Government contributed to the cost of a new link span at Douglas. The chosen vessel was the two year old, 2,753 ton 'Monte Castillo', built for an England to Canary Island service which had failed. It was renamed 'Manx Viking'.

The new service was dogged with problems. The start up was delayed from 1 June 1978 until 26 August. After only a fortnight, 'Manx Viking' was out of action for mechanical repairs. Then on 1 December 1978 the link span at Douglas was virtually destroyed in a storm. It looked as though Manx Line would go the way of earlier attempts to

The 'Manx Viking' entering Heysham from Douglas on 17 June 1979, still in original Manx Line livery.
(Peter Sunderland)

The 13.00 'boat train' leaving Heysham for Stockport on 16 May 1987. The signal box opened with the replacement station in 1970 but closed in 1986. *(Tom Heavyside)*

142048 at Heysham on 26 September 1995. *(F.W. Smith)*

ne of six classic steamers uilt for the Isle of Man Steam acket Company after the econd World War, 'Mona's sle' is seen at Douglas on 26 ay 1974. Three months later, worked the final sailing to eysham.
(Martin Bairstow)

A Derby built dmu has worked into Heysham as the Isle of Man Boat Train from Stockport on 23 May 1987.
(Martin Bairstow)

ynwald', the former 'Antrim rincess' entering Douglas arbour from Heysham in ay 1987. *(Martin Bairstow)*

break the monopoly of the Steam Packet.

But Manx Line was taken over by Sealink, then still a subsidiary of British Railways. 'Manx Viking' resumed the service in May 1979 and became very successful. Making two return trips a day and carrying passengers, cars and lorries, it was doing business for which the Steam Packet would have required at least three ships. It was from the Steam Packet that most of the traffic was transferring. The total market was not expanding.

By the end of 1984, the Steam Packet faced liquidation. Earlier that year, Sealink had been privatised into the hands of Sea Containers. They rescued the Steam Packet by taking a 40% shareholding which effectively gave control as the other 60% was held very diversely. The two services merged with Heysham becoming the main English terminal from 1 April 1985. For a time, Liverpool was abandoned altogether as an Isle of Man port.

The advantages of Heysham over Liverpool included ownership by Sealink, a shorter crossing, no locks, lower port charges, fewer strikes and easier motorway access. A bus connection was provided from Lancaster station. A rail service to Heysham was reintroduced on 11 May 1987 but only in connection with the daytime sailing which arrives Heysham at 12.30 and leaves at 14.15.

Although it was Manx Line which had baled out its competitor, the amalgamated operation was still marketed as the Isle of Man Steam Packet. They didn't want to abandon a company with a 155 year pedigree. The immediate result was a fiasco. The couldn't dispose of the freight vessel 'Peveril' sc they sacrificed the multi purpose 'Manx Viking instead. The new flagship was the 'Mona Isle', 4,65 tons, built in 1966 as Townsend-Thoresen's 'Fre Enterprise III'. It lasted only a few months durin which it had great difficulty navigating int Heysham, sometimes missing, occasionall damaging the port facilities. It was replaced b Sealink's 'Antrim Princess' from the Stranraer–Larn route which was renamed 'Tynwald', the sixth vesse to carry this traditional Manx name.

When Sea Containers sold most of Sealink t Stena Line in 1990, they retained their interests i Heysham and the Isle of Man. In 1997 Se Containers acquired complete ownership of the Isl of Man Steam Packet which in August 199 introduced the brand new 'Ben-My-Chree' onto th Heysham–Douglas service. This took over both th passenger/car ferry and freight business.

The 'Ben-My-Chree' sails all year round fron Heysham to Douglas, generally at 02.15 and 14.15. carries 500 passengers and 175 vehicles. It is a Ro-Pa vessel designed for heavy lorry traffic hence th relatively low passenger capacity. The Compan again caters for much of the Isle of Man passenge and car ferry business via Liverpool using a 'Seacat high speed vessel. During mid Summer 2000, high speed ship will also provide extra Heysham t Douglas sailings on up to three days per week.

'Ben My Chree' leaving Heysham for Douglas in March 2000. *(Martin Bairstow)*

The 'Channel Entente' arriving at Douglas from Heysham on 2 August 1990. The former train ferry was renamed 'King Orry' later in 1990. To the left is the 'Mona's Queen'. *(Stuart Baker)*

A Company with tradition. Window on the 'King Orry' 1993. *(John Holroyd)*

Freight tonnage at Heysham, 29 June 1998. 'Riverdance' (left) is on the Warrenpoint service, 'Merchant Bravery' on the Belfast. *(John Holroyd)*

Locomotives on Shed

By F. W. Smith

Skipton

The first engine shed at Skipton, erected in 1850, was of wooden construction. A replacement three road shed, built in 1877, was also of wood. A second similar structure plus a new coaling stage were added in 1892. No turntable was available at the shed until a 60ft vacuum operated table was brought into use in 1939. Previously locos had to be turned on a 46ft table at the south end of the station.

By the late 1940s the wooden buildings were in a woebegone state, most of the roofs being non-existent. In the early 1950s BR decided something must be done and the entire depot was rebuilt in brick and concrete. Coded 30 in late Midland and early LMS days, Skipton became 20F in 1935. It was changed briefly to 23A in 1950/51 and then 24G in 1957. This lasted until September 1963 when it became 10G. The shed was closed on 3 April 1967 but the building is still used by the local authority.

The 1920 allocation was 22 locomotives comprising eleven 2-4-0s and the same number of 4-4-0s but no freight engines!

The October 1951 allocation was 34 engines mainly freight.

My visit on Sunday 3 July 1955 found the following on shed:

1F	0-6-0T	Midland	41855
3F	0-6-0T	LMS	47428, 47562
2	2-6-2T		41273, 41326
3	2-6-2T		40140
2P	4-4-0	Midland	40414/72
2P	4-4-0	LMS	40602
2	2-6-0		46442
3F	0-6-0		43257/95
4	2-6-0		43112
4P	4-4-0	LMS	41100
4F	0-6-0	Midland	43893, 43913/16/60, 44007
4F	0-6-0	LMS	44222/77
5	2-6-0	'Crab'	42877
5	4-6-0		44660, 44792
8F	2-8-0		48469
Total 25			

Skipton Shed, April 1959. 8F No. 48105 is flanked by two 4Fs. 43960 on the right. *(Jim Davenport)*

Ex L&Y Class 2P 2-4-2T No. 10671 at Skipton shed in 1948. Coal covers the rear windows. It was withdrawn in March 1952. *(F.W. Smith)*

Skipton 1946. 4F 0-6-0 No. 3999, 1F 0-6-0T No. 1751 and 2P 4-4-0 No. 359 stored out of use in a siding near the station. 1751 probably never worked again as it was officially withdrawn in July 1946. *(F.W. Smith)*

Ex Midland 2F 0-6-0 No. 3477 at Skipton shed in 1949. Built in 1896, it was withdrawn in March 1950, never having gained a BR number. *(F.W. Smith)*

Hellifield

A new engine shed at Hellifield was planned in 1879 and was more or less completed by the end of the following year.

It was a four road straight shed with twin roof pitches. It was situated just to the north of the station. A larger coaling stage was provided. Unusually this was constructed entirely in wood. The 1910 allocation was 28 engines.

The Lancashire & Yorkshire Railway also had an engine shed at Hellifield, opened in 1881 on its own territory alongside the Blackburn line. When the L&Y shed closed in 1927, its engines and men transferred to the Midland.

Two large wooden wedge snowploughs were a feature at Hellifield. They were required frequently during the terrible winters on the Settle & Carlisle line. In Midland days Hellifield was a sub shed of Skipton, coded 30A. In 1935 it became 20G and by the end of the Second World War had an allocation of some 30 locomotives. A new 60ft turntable was installed in 1940 replacing the old unit and in 1948 a new repair shop and wheel drop were constructed at the rear of the shed bringing welcome additional work. Hellifield briefly became 23B in 1950 but reverted to 20G in 1951. In March 1957 it became 24H in the Accrington District and was finally closed on 17 June 1963. Two years later it was used for storing preserved engines including LNER V2 2-6-2 No.4771 'Green Arrow', Midland 2-4-0 No.158A, Midland 4-2-2 No.118 and London, Tilbury & Southend 4-4-2T No.80. After their departure it became abandoned and derelict before final demolition.

My visit on Sunday 3 July 1955 found the following engines on shed:

LMS	3	2-6-2T	40120/62/63/83/84
LMS	2	2-6-2T	41206
Mid	3F	0-6-0	43585
L&Y	3F	0-6-0	52526
LMS	4F	0-6-0	44149/81, 44276/82, 44579
LMS	2P	4-4-0	40632
LMS	5	2-6-0	42770/84
LMS	5	4-6-0	44934
LMS	6	4-6-0	45665
LMS	8F	2-8-0	48105, 48612
WD		2-8-0	90354

Total 21

Stored at Hellifield for eventual display at the National Railway Museum, ex Great Eastern Railway Class J17 0-6-0 No. 1217 (BR No. 65567). *(David Beeken)*

'Jubilee' 4-6-0 No. 45705 'Seahorse' terminating at Hellifield with the 8.05 all stations from Carlisle. 'Crab' 2-6-0 No. 42907 shunts the shed yard on an inclement 24 September 1963. *(Peter E. Baughan)*

45622 'Nyasaland' passing Hellifield North Junction and loco shed with a northbound express in July 1963. 44856 is travelling the other way. *(Peter Sunderland)*

Lancaster Green Ayre

Lancaster Green Ayre Shed on 17 March 1962 with 'Jubilee' Class No. 45675 'Hardy', 'Patriot' Class Nos. 45505 'The Royal Army Ordnance Corps', 45507 'Royal Tank Corps' and 8F No. 48622.
(P. B. Booth/N. E. Stead Collection)

It appears that the first shed at Green Ayre opened with the line from Skipton in 1850. It comprised a small brick building near the station which lasted until the 1930s. By 1857 it was agreed that a much larger facility was required and a start was made on the new shed which had four roads and a single bay workshop. The site was somewhat cramped and the only access was via the turntable. The shed roof was renewed in 1933 but the workshop closed at that time. In 1937 a new 60ft vacuum operated turntable was installed.

Lancaster was Midland shed No.32. It became 11C under the ex LNW shed at Carnforth in 1935. In 1936 it was transferred back to the Leeds district becoming 20H. In 1950 for a short time it became 23C under Skipton but in September 1951 was recoded 11E once more under Carnforth. This lasted until March 1957 when it was placed under Accrington as 24J. Its final code was 10J from September 1963 until closure which took place on 18 April 1966.

In the early days the locomotives allocated were mainly 2-4-0s and 0-6-0s, the 1879 allocation being four 2-4-0s and four 0-6-0s and a solitary 2-2-2. Passenger work to Skipton, Leeds and Bradford were the most important runs. The 2-4-0s were gradually replaced by 4-4-0s, the last being Johnson No.213 in 1933.

On 4 February 1934, the former London & North Western shed at Lancaster was closed. This had been situated just south of Castle Station. Most of its work was transferred to Green Ayre along with staff and some locomotives. This generated a flow of light engine movements between Castle and Green Ayre. Sometimes they ran coupled together to minimise occupation of the single line section.

On 30 March 1940, engines on Green Ayre shed were:

2P	4-4-0	Mid	455, 558
4P	4-4-0	LMS	929, 931
4P	2-6-4T	LMS	2361
4F	0-6-0	LMS	4227, 4291, 4553
3F	0-6-0T	LMS	7468

The down Bradford FS to Morecambe 'Residential Express' was worked that day by compound No.930 from Holbeck shed.

My visit on Sunday 3 July 1955 found the following on shed:

2P	0-4-4T	LMS	41900/03/04
3F	0-6-0T	Mid	47201
3F	0-6-0T	LMS	47468/70, 47532, 47639
4	2-6-4T		42135/36
4P	4-4-0	LMS	41045/65.41107/08, 41152/96/97
5	2-6-0		42888
4	2-6-0		43113
4F	0-6-0	Mid	43944
4F	0-6-0	LMS	44468
3F	0-6-0		43271
8F	2-8-0		48276/83
WD	2-8-0		90364
Total 25			

The 0-4-4 tanks were push-pull fitted for the

Lancaster–Morecambe–Heysham passenger trains during interruptions to the electric service in 1951-53 and 1955-56. Two of them, 41903/4 were still at Green Ayre, stored out of use in June 1960.

At this latter date, Green Ayre's allocation included diesel shunters D3867 and D3871. They were rarely seen at Lancaster because they stabled overnight where they were employed at Heysham Harbour.

The allocation in 1920 was:

2-4-0	209, 210, 211, 213
0-6-0T	1659, 1680, 1681
0-4-4T	1266/68/69/70/71, 1411/12/13/14/15/17/30
0-6-0	2404/37/55/56/58/68/75/84/85 93, 2504/06/07/98, 2707
0-6-0	2914, 3036/37/38/39, 3188/89, 3237, 3314/33/45/46/47/50/51/53/54/57/58/59/87/89/90, 3410, 3429/53, 3502, 3680.

Total 62

Green Ayre Shed stood alongside the Castle branch on the left of the photo. An electric unit is approaching Green Ayre from Castle. The line to Morecambe curves to the right over the Greyhound Bridge, 28 December 1965. *(Geoffrey Lewthwaite)*

Carnforth Midland Shed No. 31

This was a roundhouse of the square type opened in 1874. It replaced a smaller building which was later used for wagon repairs. The shed stood on the north side of the Wennington line and in 1920 had a substantial allocation of 62 locomotives. The majority of these were 0-6-0s employed on freight from the Furness area towards Leeds and Bradford. Passenger traffic was looked after by a small number of 2-4-0s and a larger quantity of 0-4-4Ts. At the Grouping Carnforth was put under control of the Western District. It went out of use in 1944 after opening of the enlarged LMS shed alongside Carnforth station.

The building still stands in private use. It is passed by trains from Leeds on the right hand side just before they cross over the Main Line.

The occupants of Carnforth Midland shed on 23 March 1940 were:

3F	0-6-0		3207(11A), 3314(11A), 3476(20B)
4F	0-6-0		4474(25E), 4510(11A)
2P	4-4-0		426(20A)
3F	0-6-0T		7409(11A)
2P	2-4-2T	Ex L&Y	10746(11A)
	0-8-0	Ex L&Y	12782(20D)

No.12782 had worked in that morning on a Stourton to Barrow coke train which changed engines at Carnforth at 10.00am. The loco remained at the Midland shed until 6.00pm the same day when it returned on the Barrow to Stourton goods. These trains were more usually worked by a Stanier 2-8-0 or an ex Midland 3F 0-6-0 from Royston or Normanton sheds.

Black Five No. 44871 'Sovereign' at Carnforth on 8 September 1988. *(F.W. Smith)*

The Future

Other books in this series have tried to dispel the notion that train services today are but a shadow of what they were in some supposed golden age. On many routes, today's regular interval trains are of an intensity out of all proportion to previous more complicated timetables. There may not be as many train movements in total because of fewer freight and parcel trains and there certainly aren't as many light engines moving around.

The 'Little' North Western is an exception to this general rule. Even the basic year round passenger service is less frequent than it used to be. Gone completely is all other traffic. From Settle Junction to Carnforth, there are just the five daily passenger trains, nearly always formed of two car diesel multiple units offering a rather slow journey.

There has been an upsurge in traffic between Skipton and Settle Junction. The Lancaster to Morecambe branch is reasonably busy. The weak link is the middle part of the route between Settle Junction and Carnforth. It is difficult to see how things can improve. The line starts in the major conurbation of West Yorkshire with connections from all over the country. But where does it lead? Since the early 1980s it has been accepted that Lancaster is the main destination. Otherwise we're left with a seaside resort which is no longer a mass market venue.

Traffic for Carlisle and Scotland nearly all goes via Appleby. Penrith and the Northern Lake District are all but impossible to reach. Since 1995, the timetable leaflet has shown connections to Windermere via Lancaster. Through journey time is typically 2 hours 40 minutes to 3 hours of which up to an hour is spent between first arriving Carnforth and speeding through the same place again. The number of passengers making this journey is small.

Connections for Barrow and other Furness Line stations are poor. Typical waits are 40 to 50 minutes at Carnforth where there are no facilities whatsoever or you can while away some of the time by travelling into and out of Lancaster.

Southbound connections at Lancaster are also typically poor but there is little demand for these anyway. Passengers from Leeds and Bradford have an hourly service direct to Preston. Those from Shipley and Keighley will find it easier to travel via Bradford.

There used to be 'boat train' business to Heysham but for the Isle of Man this is impossible from the 'Little' North Western line. The 10.17 ex Leeds will connect at either Lancaster or Morecambe with the 'boat train' to Heysham but there is no service the other way. The return 'boat train' misses a Leeds connection by 30 minutes and there is not another for 3½ hours.

The Belfast ferry reopened without a boat train but a connection from Lancaster and Morecambe is provided in the May 2000 timetable. The 8.17 from Leeds will catch the 12.00 ship whilst the 11.00 arrival from Belfast allows time to get the 13.07 train from Lancaster.

This development apart, the 'Little' North Western remains something of a backwater. It is not easy to see an answer. Perhaps the most promising destination would be Windermere. There has been some suggestion of a through train from Leeds to 'Trans Pennine Express' standard. This is physically impossible without increasing the capacity of the Oxenholme to Windermere branch which is fully occupied with its present service.

During November 1999, Leeds–Carlisle trains were diverted via Carnforth due to engineering work on the direct route. They reversed at Carnforth (not Lancaster) and gave a direct service to Penrith not seen since LMS days. Maybe, if the through Leeds to Glasgow service is expanded from its present one train per day, some could go via Carnforth, Oxenholme and Penrith.

There is a possibility that the local authority may apply for Government funding for an enhanced local service between Skipton and Lancaster. This would be aimed partly at commuters into Lancaster who at present have no arrival between 6.43 and 10.05. It is difficult to know whether there would be sufficient demand from 'Little' North Western stations. If only the route were direct from Wennington, the train would be faster and could pick up at Caton and Halton.

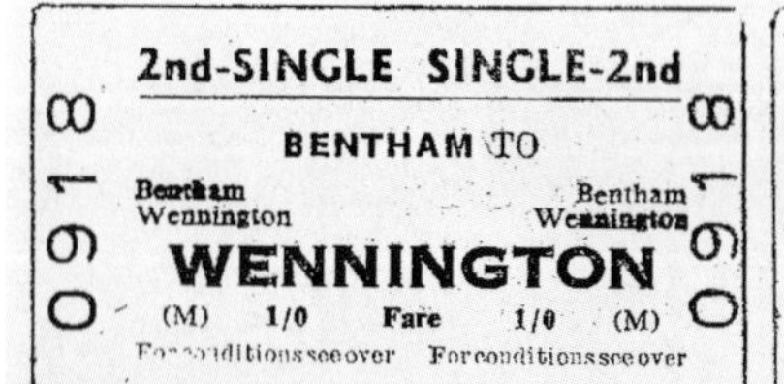

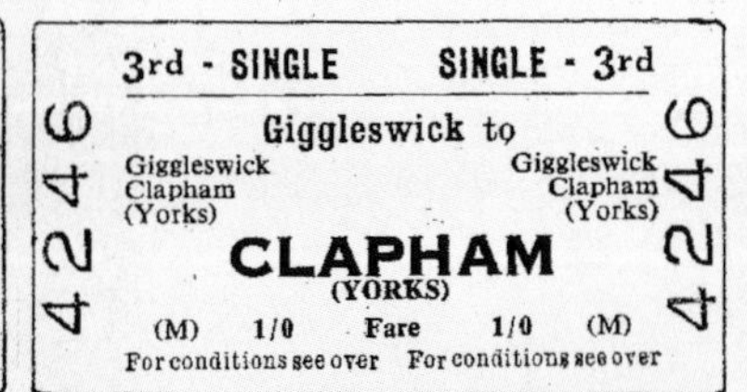

Conclusion

When it came to route rationalisation in the 1960s the wrong lines were sometimes selected for retention and abandonment.

There is a strong argument that the best route from Leeds to Carlisle would have been via Clapham and Low Gill rather than Settle Junction to Carlisle. No deliberate choice was ever made in favour of the latter. In 1966 they intended to eliminate both. It just happened that Clapham to Low Gill was the easiest to dispense with first.

In the case of Wennington to Morecambe, the decision to route via Carnforth was deliberate and based on prevailing freight traffic. That has long since disappeared and the line survives purely for a passenger business which would definitely be better had the alternative been retained. Wennington–Lancaster Green Ayre–Castle would be direct and offer more intermediate potential. It would have a more convenient station in Lancaster and involve no conflicting movements on the West Coast Main Line.

Between Lancaster and Morecambe, there are arguments in favour of both routes. The imperatives seem to have been to eradicate electric working and free the Greyhound Bridge for use as a road. If the LNWR branch was the best choice, they never completed the job by reopening Euston Road and building the direct curve to Heysham.

The optimum would have been Midland from Wennington to Lancaster and LNW into Morecambe. Leeds–Morecambe trains would have served both Lancaster stations. Morecambe locals could have started at Green Ayre, reversing at Castle.

Is it too far fetched to imagine that one day it will be an embarrassment to have Leeds–Morecambe trains fouling up 150mph schedules on the West Coast Main Line? Of the 11 miles between Wennington and Lancaster Castle, the first 5½ are in open country. The remaining 5½ are in use as a footpath/cycle track. The double track formation is wide enough to accommodate the latter alongside a single line railway.

'Jinty' 3F No. 47662 at the east end of Lancaster Green Ayre Station on 24 September 1963. The Skirton Bridge was then the only road crossing of the River Lune so they coveted the railway viaduct to create a second road bridge. *(Peter E. Baughan)*

There is now talk of a commuter service from the Skipton line into Lancaster. What a pity that the route takes a time consuming detour avoiding the places which might offer some traffic such as Halton seen from a stopping train, also on 24 September 1963. *(Peter E. Baughan)*

Appendix

Opened

12. 6.1848 Lancaster GA – Morecambe
30. 7.1849 Skipton – Ingleton
17.11.1849 Wennington – Lancaster GA
18.12.1849 Lancaster GA – Castle
2. 5.1850 Bentham – Wennington
1. 6.1850 Clapham – Bentham
24. 8.1861 Ingleton – Low Gill (goods)
16. 9.1861 Ingleton – Low Gill (passenger)

Closed to Passengers

30. 1.1954 Clapham – Low Gill
2. 1.1966 Wennington – Morecambe
2. 1.1966 Lancaster GA – Castle
4.10.1975 Morecambe – Heysham (reopened 11.5.1987)

Closed to all Traffic

18. 6.1966 Clapham – Low Gill
4. 6.1967 Wennington – Ladies Walk
4. 6.1967 Green Ayre – White Lund
4. 6.1967 Torrisholme No.1 – Morecambe
31. 1.1970 White Lund – Torrisholme No.2
16. 3.1976 Ladies Walk – Lancaster Castle

A number of stations were resited including Skipton, Hellifield, Carnforth, Morecambe and Heysham

Miles	Stations	Opened	Closed
0	Skipton	7. 9.1847	–
3 3/4	Gargrave	30. 7.1849	–
6 1/2	Bell Busk	30. 7.1849	2. 5.1959
10	Hellifield	30. 7.1849	–
11 1/4	Long Preston	30. 7.1849	–
13 1/4	Settle Junction	10.11.1876	31.10.1877
15	Giggleswick	30. 7.1849	–
21 3/4	Clapham	30. 7.1849	–
26	Ingleton (M)	30. 7.1849	30. 1.1954
26 1/2	Ingleton (LNW)	16. 9.1861	31.12.1916
31	Kirkby Lonsdale	16. 9.1861	30. 1.1954
34	Barbon	16. 9.1861	30. 1.1954
36 3/4	Middleton on Lune	16. 9.1861	11. 4.1931
40 1/2	Sedbergh	16. 9.1861	30. 1.1954
44 3/4	Low Gill	16. 9.1861	5. 3.1960
25	Bentham	2. 5.1850	–
28 1/4	Wennington	17.11.1849	–
29 3/4	Melling	6. 6.1867	3. 5.1952
31	Arkholme	6. 6.1867	10. 9.1960
34 3/4	Borwick	6. 6.1867	10. 9.1960
37 3/4	Carnforth	22. 9.1846	–
30 1/2	Hornby	17.11.1849	15. 9.1957
34 1/2	Caton	17.11.1849	30. 4.1961
36 1/4	Halton	17.11.1849	2. 1.1966
38 3/4	Lancaster Green Ayre	12. 6.1848	2. 1.1966
39 1/2	Lancaster Castle	22. 9.1846	–
39 3/4	Scale Hall	8. 6.1957	2. 1.1966
42 1/4	Morecambe	12. 6.1848	–
44 1/2	Middleton Road	1. 9.1904	12. 4.1908
45 1/2	Heysham	1. 9.1904	4. 10.1975 (reopened 11. 5.1987)

LNWR Morecambe Branch
Opened

13. 8.1864 Hest Bank – Morecambe
19. 5.1888 M South Jn – Bare Lane

Miles	Stations	Opened	Closed
0	Hest Bank	22. 9.1846	4.11.1967
1	Bare Lane	13. 8.1864	–
2	Morecambe Poulton Lane	13. 8.1864	8. 5.1886
2 1/4	Morecambe Euston Road	9. 5.1886	8. 9.1962

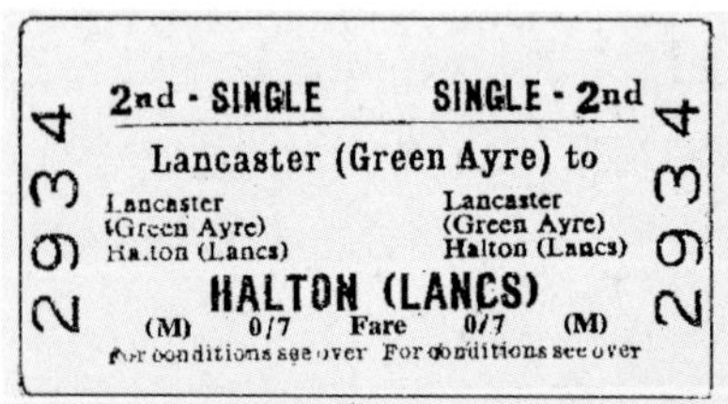

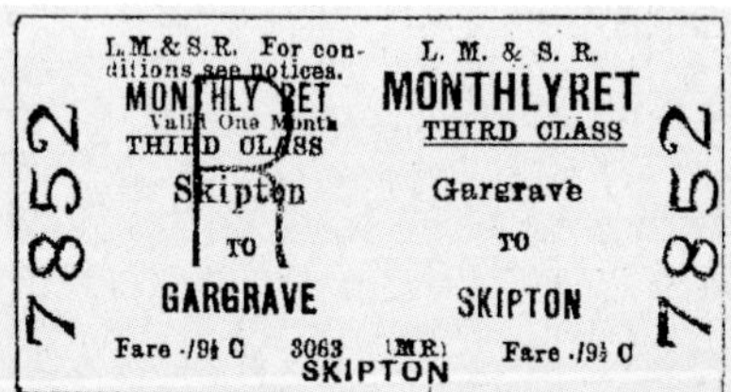

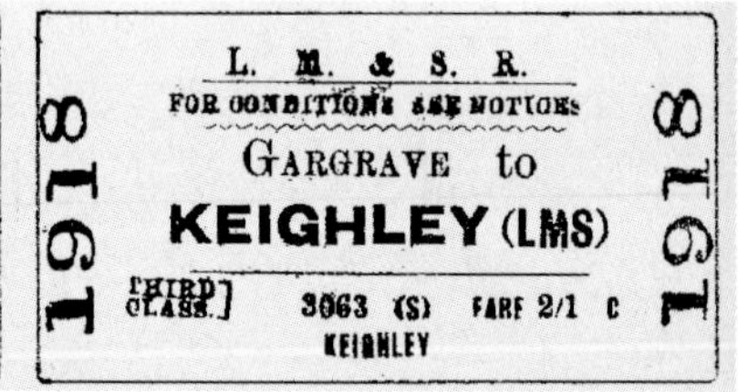

A special word of thanks is due to Peter Sunderland who has a long standing interest in Lancaster, Morecambe and Heysham. Here Peter is in charge of the 'Adrian Special' from Morecambe to Lancaster by the Midland route. A come down maybe for someone who remembers the 'Belfast Boat Express' and the 'Residential'.

Will Adrian (born 1998) one day look at a light rapid transit system and say 'I went on that in my pushchair before it became a railway'.

(Martin Bairstow)

72007 'Clan Mackintosh' at Lancaster Green Ayre on 25 May 1964. None of the ten 'Clans' were preserved but the Swanage Railway is building a new one. *(Martin Bairstow Collection)*

M 1041

L M S

LONDON MIDLAND AND SCOTTISH RAILWAY.

SPRING and EARLY SUMMER HOLIDAY RETURN TICKETS, 1931.

TO

NORTHERN IRELAND

FRIDAYS and SATURDAYS,
April 10th up to and including July 18th,

EXCURSION TICKETS TO

ANTRIM	CASTLEROCK	NEWCASTLE (CO. DOWN)
ARDGLASS	COLERAINE	NEWTOWNARDS
ARMAGH	DONAGHADEE	PORTSTEWART
BALLYCASTLE	DOWNPATRICK	PORTRUSH
BALLYMENA	ENNISKILLEN	WARRENPOINT
BANGOR	GIANT'S CAUSEWAY	WHITEHEAD, &c.
BELFAST	LARNE	
CARRICKFERGUS	LONDONDERRY	

SATURDAYS, APRIL 11th up to and including JULY 18th,

To LONDONDERRY only

(Via HEYSHAM and DIRECT BOAT.)

CHOICE OF TWO ROUTES BY L.M.S. STEAMERS.

Via HEYSHAM & BELFAST.— Open Sea Passage, 6 Hours 15 Minutes.
Via STRANRAER & LARNE. — Open Sea Passage, 2 Hours 10 Minutes.
BOOKINGS ALSO VIA LIVERPOOL AND BELFAST STEAMSHIP COMPANY.

PASSENGERS ARE REQUESTED TO OBTAIN THEIR TICKETS IN ADVANCE.

CONDITIONS OF ISSUE OF EXCURSION AND OTHER REDUCED FARE TICKETS.
Excursion Tickets, and Tickets issued at Fares less than the Ordinary Fares, are issued subject to the Notices and Conditions shown in the Company's current Time Tables.

PLEASE RETAIN THIS BILL FOR REFERENCE.
M 1041

ISBN 1-87-1944-21X
9 781871 944211